D1550598

PERSONHOOD

Other books by Leo Buscaglia

Love
Because I Am Human
The Way of the Bull
The Disabled and Their Parents: A Counseling Challenge
Living, Loving & Learning
The Fall of Freddie the Leaf

PERSONHOOD

The Art of Being Fully Human

by Leo Buscaglia, Ph.D.

Published by Charles B. Slack, Inc.
Distributed by Holt, Rinehart and Winston

Library of Congress Catalog Card Number: 78-66423
Charles B. Slack, Inc. ISBN: 0-913590-63-0
Holt, Rinehart and Winston ISBN: 0-03-063202-1

Published in the United States of America by Charles B. Slack, Inc.,
6900 Grove Road, Thorofare, New Jersey 08086

In the United States, distributed to the trade by Holt, Rinehart
and Winston, 383 Madison Avenue, New York, New York 10017

In Canada, distributed by Holt, Rinehart and Winston, Limited,
55 Horner Avenue, Toronto, Ontario M8Z 4X0 Canada

4   6   8   10   9   7   5

Charles B. Slack, Inc.   ISBN 0-913590-63-0

Holt, Rinehart and Winston ISBN 0-03-063202-1

This book is dedicated to those who are eager to encounter themselves before their death

therefore

it is dedicated to LIFE and those HUMAN BEINGS who strive to give it their special meaning.

Table of Contents

The self that we are now contains the actualization potential which will fulfill us.

I realize today that nothing in the world is more distasteful to a man than to take the path that leads to himself.

Herman Hesse
Demian

As early as the Sixth Century B.C. a very humane philosopher, Kung-fu-tze (Confucious), lamented,

Why does the world create cares for itself? All roads lead to the same place. All thoughts go to the same conclusions. Why does the world create cares for itself?

This very human question continues to resound disturbingly in the minds of all of us as we engage in the daily processes of living. What is most disillusioning is that we seem to have come no closer to an answer over these thousands of years. Rather, we have persisted in abusing and killing ourselves and each other. More and more we appear to be losing the joy in spontaneity and the wonder in spirituality. We seem to have become alienated from the fact that we are all part of everything and everyone, and we have retreated into egocentricity and provincialism. As a result, we, and the world in which we live, still are mainly unrealized potential. We are all much less than what we can be.

Existence is like an intricate tapestry on which no part can remain unrealized if we are to experience the sublime totality. In this sense no one life is of more or less significance than another nor is any one of us more or less responsible, for in each of us lies a vital part of the wholeness. Unless we *all* assume the responsibility of actualizing our lives by living as fully functioning persons, we will perpetuate the long history and irreclaimable loss of possibility which alone can consummate the picture. We will continue to create cares for ourselves and others, and Confucious' question will persist.

This work is but a meager attempt at celebrating personhood, that very human state which alone, if lived fully and actively, can truly actualize the beauty, strength and meaning of existence. Because of the vastness and grandeur of its subject, this short statement will appear to many as being insignificant, vague and frustratingly incomplete. It is probably all of these things.

Also, the more I learn about people and the world in which I live, the more incapable I seem to be of expressing to others what I have learned. Thus what is written may seem to be elementary and repetitious. Finally, since I desire strongly to communicate with as many people as may show interest, to write as a scholar even if I were able to do so would have limited my perspective. I may therefore be accused of having used an insultingly simplistic style. So be it. In addition, I frankly admit that this work will reflect my personal bias, feelings and values. It will unabashedly reveal my natural love, respect and optimism for personkind and my excitement and hope for our future. It is written as a start, a challenge for people on the road to self-discovery, self-respect, personal development, change and actualization. It is intended only as a small, fragile seed dropped in the wind. A possible beginning. It will either grow or die depending upon where it falls and how it is nurtured.

Loren Eiseley describes our world as a place "where even a spider refuses to lie down and die if a rope can still be spun to a star."

Like the spider, there are those of us who refuse to stop spinning, even when it would appear to be far more sophisticated to be without hope. Our rope, though perhaps frail, can still be spun with optimism, curiosity, wonder, love and the sincere desire to share a trip to the stars. Our goal is worth the struggle, for in this case, the star to which we aspire is full humanity for all.

I feel strongly that in the continual striving for the actualization of every living thing lies our only hope. This is the unique challenge of Personhood and the sole purpose of this book.

INTRODUCTION

Down how many roads among the stars must
man propel himself in search of the final
secret? The journey is difficult, immense,
at times impossible, yet that will not
deter some of us from attempting it. . . .
We have joined the caravan, you might say,
at a certain point; we will travel as far
as we can, but we cannot in one lifetime
see all that we would like to see or to
learn all that we hunger to know.—

Loren Eiseley
The Immense Journey

Life is an "immense journey" and each of us has only one lifetime to travel it. We will wind our own way continuously and relentlessly molding, growing, remodifying our undefined course, performing acts we can never redo on a path we can never retrace. Each moment moves us imperceptibly closer to the journey's end, so that when finally reached, it appears to be simply a vague, cluttered memory in our mind — inexplicable, like an interrupted dream, felt, but half forgotten, and seemingly without purpose.

Yet all of us will take our unique journey.

My personal journey has been a good one. It has brought me through a childhood of wonder, an adolescence of painful but exciting revelation and an adulthood which has solidified

1

my life. It has given me a meaningful vocation which has been my greatest joy and which has opened up a myriad of viable and challenging opportunities. It has taken me to every state in the Union and every continent in the world. It has afforded me the opportunity to share knowledge and wisdom with children as well as aged scholars.

It has brought me into intimate social contact with cultures of striking differences and human persons from peasants in remote tropical villages to world-wise sophisticates in complicated cultures.

On a hot orange afternoon, traveling on a bus in southern India, I saw a woman. She was clad in a faded sari and walking away from the road, erect, strong and determined. Firmly balanced on her head was a large, heavy water pot. The desert about her was vast. There was no sign of where she had been and less indication of where she was going, unless she was carrying water to the sunset. She paused for a moment and our eyes met. We *knew* each other.

A beautiful, toothless old farmer in Nepal once put me up for the night in his home. It was a thatched hut which housed his family, farming equipment and all of his animals. Conversation, beyond sign language, a smile, eye contact, a touch, was impossible. He had no idea where America was, had never spoken to a Westerner, nor had he traveled in a car. He had heard nothing of history, had no concern for politics, or, for that matter, anything beyond his village life. Still, for an evening we were brought warmly together. When the time for parting came, feeling that we would probably never meet again, we walked arm in arm to the village's end and wept. We are still together.

A young, anxious businessman helped me to find my way on a busy, smoggy and humid Tokyo afternoon. He went miles off his busy path to direct me to the address I was seeking. In the short period we were together we hardly spoke. We finally bowed in parting and he went quickly on his way. A part of me went with him.

A teenager in Brooklyn, New York, came enthusiastically to me after a lecture with a joyous gleam in his eye. He announced firmly that I had helped him in his rebellion and that it now had a cause — that cause was preserving his own potential! We shared our common goal with a warm embrace. I wonder about him still.

A kindergarten child, in whose classroom I had taught, once looked at me strangely as I was stacking my tray with food in the school cafeteria and asked, "Do you eat?" She delighted in my roar of laughter! We knew joy together and I relive that joy as I retell the tale.

For these few brief seconds of our encounters, I was and still am that Indian woman, that Nepalese farmer, that Japanese businessman, that New York student, that kindergarten child. We were all one in the same thing, humanness. When our minds could not meet, our hearts were the common bond. When our speech was a mystery, it was solved by our eyes and arms.

All those people I have met, no matter the difference, were uniquely engaged, more or less successfully, in taking their immense journey. Some moved in technological wonder, others in primitive magic; some rested in material opulence, others in the greatest simplicity and even desperate poverty; some were equipped with strong formal educations, others simply used their natural mental endowments, enriched by experience. But, whatever, they all had a strong common tie — their humanness, their deep need to survive, to realize their experience, to love and be loved, to overcome loneliness and isolation, to use their creative endeavors to make things more comfortable and beautiful for themselves and their loved ones, to attempt to understand their world and their part in it. All of them shared that singular universal commonality, that of impending death. Willingly or unwillingly, each person was obliged to accept the challenge of his or her personal voyage, equipped, as it were, with what they were, knowing they would come to the same end.

It was apparent that many succeeded. They seemed to be in touch with their unique humanness, and it was enough. Others failed.

Each of these people were the history of all people, but all were also a part of the unique history which only their lives would write. For in each of them and the world in which they lived, there was far more future than past. It was their personhood that, at each moment, was creating and recreating the world.

Were any of us any less human persons because our lives were more or less complicated, civilized or separate? Was their way as valid as mine? Was Confucius correct in postulating that our thoughts would arrive at the same conclusions and our roads lead to the same place, no matter the way?

For centuries people like ourselves, as well as great religious leaders, philosophers, scientists and educators, have studied and reflected upon man's continuing search for the human answers to these questions.

Abraham Maslow lamented that the process was "devilishly difficult to pursue through scientific study" but nevertheless, he did much to dignify the questioning and state the answers in human language. He described the universality of humanity, the commonality of our experiences, attempts at self-realization, our being needs, our deficiency needs. In his lifetime, he produced an abundance of scientific evidence regarding our "special inner life" as human beings. Throughout his life, he continued to puzzle about why some of us were able to become what we are and why others did not seem to "make it."

He stated,

Only a small portion of the human population gets to the point of identity, or of selfhood, full humanness, self-actualization, etc., even in a society like ours which is relatively one of the most fortunate on the face of the earth. This is the great paradox. We have the impulse toward full development of humanness. Then why is it that it doesn't happen more often?[1]

5

The following chapters will celebrate universal humanness. They will attempt to offer an historic view of the ethical principles which have guided our humanity. They will also look at what it might entail to live in full humanness in our society today. Finally, they will present the ultimate challenge to those of us who are eager to experience ourselves and our lives as fully as possible before our death. So that we may perhaps avoid what the great religious leader, Mahatma Gandhi warned us about in his Autobiography,

> I am familiar with the superstition that self realization is possible only in the fourth stage of life, i.e., sannyasa (renunciation). But it is a matter of common knowledge that those who defer preparation for this invaluable experience until the last stage of life attain not self realization but old age amounting to a second and pitiable childhood, living as a burden on this earth.[2]

THE START

But where was I to start? The world is so vast, I shall start with the country I know best, my own. But my country is so very large. I had better start with my town. But my town, too, is large. I had best start with my street. No: my home. No: my family. Never mind, I shall start with myself.

Elie Wiesel
Souls on Fire

CHAPTER 1

At birth we are given the greatest gift — life — and as our first birthday present, we are presented with a fantastic world in which to live. These gifts, though we may often depreciate and abuse them, will always be our most real and valuable possessions. Even so, as Thoreau noted in *Walden*, most of us will have so little respect for life that we will reach the point of death without ever having lived at all. Erich Fromm echoed this fear when he stated that the greatest tragedy in life was the fact that most human beings died before they were fully born.

My mother and father lived instinctively in the knowledge that life and living were arts to be celebrated. From outward appearances, they would seem to have little reason for celebration. They were penniless Italian immigrants attempting to make a new life in a friendless foreign land. They had neither the language nor the sophistication to adapt easily to their newly chosen culture, but they took up the challenge with gusto, abandonment, love, faith and a great deal of humor.

They found a modest place to live which they painted pink with white trim and which, within a few months, became even more shockingly alive with gardens of flowers and seasonal fruits and vegetables.

The birds were the first to accept their new neighbors, for they could always count upon Papa for a fresh drink of water and some nutritious sunflower seeds on their winged way from here to there.

Mama was the gastronomic envy of all. Her gnocchi and ravioli dissolved in your mouth like puffs of meringue. Her risotto alla Milanese and polenta, which she stirred lovingly for what seemed an eternity, were masterful. The aroma of garlic, anchovies and olive oil simmering noisily in her bagna calda caused mouths to water for miles around. Her artful singing was classic. Her large, soft eyes were always full of acceptance.

Papa and Mama became neither famous nor infamous during their lifetime. They lived each day simply, beginning with a giant bowl of cafe' latte and ending with an arm-in-arm stroll through the neighborhood. They accepted tragedy and death as warmly as they did joy and birth — as simply life.

They were married for over 60 years. Mama died at 82; Papa at 86. Mama was almost as beautiful at the time of her death as she was in the lace gown of her wedding photograph. Papa was slim, active and vital at 86. His final request, after learning of his impending death, was a short trip to San Francisco's North Beach area, where he could bask in a bit of old Italy. He also requested a weekend in Las Vegas so that he could make one last attempt at breaking the bank on the five cent slot machines. Both wishes were granted.

He so loved living that even after his illness had blinded him, he was able to say, "It's all right. If I'm given a little more time, I know my way in the garden and I can still feed the birds."

I was raised in this life-filled setting. Of course, it was not always easy. There were times of tears and despair when, if it had not been for the music, the laughter, Papa's wisteria over the driveway, and Mama's delicious cabbage and stale bread torte, we might not have been able to keep body and spirit going. But my "start" was a good one which has been reinforced over the years. I learned to love. I learned to feel passionately and express it without shame. I learned to laugh. I learned to see. I learned to listen. I learned to care. I learned to take full responsibility for my world. I learned to make each day a new adventure. I learned that to take from life was a privilege and that to give my uniqueness to life was my responsibility.

The thought that my family and I had any special way of life never occurred to me. It was simply a matter of living fully as the unique human beings we were. As I grew up, I had no idea of choice, free will or self-actualization. As those around me, I had allowed myself to embrace life and the rest came naturally.

Since then, through my education, my work, and in my daily life, I have had some rude awakenings. Most people are not happy and do not expect to be so in this life. Mental health statistics continually show a frightening increase of patients in mental hospitals and outpatient clinics. There are some 300,000 people now contained in 324 county and state mental institutions in the United States. Over 200,000 individuals are being treated in outpatient clinics. Some 125,000 chronic depressives are in desperate need of treatment which is offered piecemeal or is entirely unavailable to them. It is believed that one out of every seven Americans will require some psychological treatment prior to middle age. There are more than 1,200,000 emotionally disturbed children and adolescents between the ages of 5 and 19; some are receiving token help but most are left to fare as best they can. Fifty thousand men and women commit suicide each year in America. There are eight to ten attempts for every one completed. This statistic is rising at an alarming rate. In the past, the highest suicide population was in the 65-year-old age group and above; but frighteningly, the fastest growing group now is among those in their early teens!

Divorce rates have reached such a level that modern marriage is no more than a trial-and-error, societal phenomenon, without meaning for many couples. In some states the divorce rates even exceed the marriage rates.

Child abuse has become an epidemic and is the prime cause of childhood hospitalizations. It is not uncommon to hear of parents who have beaten their children into imbecility, blinded them, burned them with cigarettes, scalded them in boiling water, or committed other atrocious crimes.

Though I should, by this time in my life, no longer be shocked by these facts, they continue to astound me. I cannot understand why, given a choice between joy and despair, people will so often choose despair. My daily experiences bring me into contact with individuals who seem totally lifeless and frighteningly apathetic. Most disturbing is their complete disrespect for their personhood. Most of them dislike themselves and where they are, and would choose, if they could, to be someone else and somewhere else. They are suspicious of others and guarded about their own selves which they keep securely buried, even though they are painfully aware of its presence. They fear risks, lack faith and scoff at hope as if it were romantic nonsense. They seem to prefer to live in constant anxiety, fear and regret. They are too frightened to live in the present and almost totally devastated by the past; too cynical to trust, and too suspicious to love. They mumble negative and bitter accusations and blame an uncaring God, neurotic parents or a sick society for placing them in a hopeless hell in which they feel helpless. They are either unaware of or unwilling to accept their potential, and take refuge in their limitations. Most of them kill time as if they had forever and never seem to seek other more viable solutions to their miserable situations.

They ignore the fact that time is running out and that no matter who they are, no one of them will get out of this world alive. They see existence as a period between an unasked-for birth and a death they live in terror of—to be lived out as painlessly as possible. They have little concern with their lifestyles or personal actualization. They engage in vague speculations regarding afterlife, reincarnation and realignment of energies, and ignore the essential reality—that they are alive now; that they have a life to live now; that whatever they are now is not all there is, but the basis for what they will have to work with in creating themselves tomorrow; that they can at any time be reborn and reorchestrate their lives to live in peace, joy and love.

It is not surprising that they avoid these insights. They have been taught so little about change and joy and growth. Life for them has always been such a vague, metaphysical condition, avoided by scientists and educators, defined for them mainly by verbose philosophers and mystic poets. The philosophical and poetic conclusions, though intriguing to some of them for some time, seem like ambiguous semantic nonsense which serve chiefly to mystify and hardly seem to reflect the "hard facts of life."

In the last two decades, the study of human life has taken a new turn. It has become the active concern of the behavioral scientists who have engaged themselves in the observation of life being lived and human behavior as it manifests itself in the daily routines of living. They have attempted to chart emotional growth, observe differing lifestyles, evaluate the quality of observable and varied emotional phenomena such as joy (Shultz); loneliness (Moustakas); courage (Tillich); isolation (Satre); love (Fromm); self-actualization (Maslow); and death (Kubler-Ross), with great practical benefits for us all. They have made us more aware of our life and death roles, of the many viable alternatives available for our choosing, and they have offered suggestions for improving the quality and style of the life we select. This has given us a whole new perspective on humanity, humans and the life choices available to all of us.

Humanist Buckminster Fuller has assured us, after over 80 years of searching, that whatever life is, it doesn't weigh anything, cannot be touched, boxed or measured upon a scale. Life, he feels, is certainly not our physical body (for we can lose forty pounds of our body and still be ourselves). The body, he says, is basically water and waste. He believes life to

14

be an awareness. The awareness of which he speaks involves much more, of course, than just comprehending. Human persons are not specialized like other primates. What makes us unique is our brain, like the brain of no other living being. The main functions of this brain are to interpret, differentiate and store significant input from the environment. The results of this activity will determine what we will refer to as our mind. Mind grows from experience perceived through the senses, and from these experiences, our personal worlds are created. As long as we remain consciously aware, we are engaged in the process of assimilating our environment and forming our lives. This is a continually active process, and we grow to the extent to which we are forced, willing or able to accommodate this onrush of new experiences. At each stage of our lives, we will be required to make personal adjustments regarding our changing world as we engage more and more in the active process of acquiring it. In this way, each of us becomes a unique patterned unit continually being regenerated as a part of a constantly changing universe. Our main challenge in this process is to uncover, develop and hold on to our unique selves. To do this will require that we be fully aware, sensitive and flexible. It will also require the keenest sense of humor. Even then it will not be an easy process. We live in complex societies, constantly surrounded by individuals who themselves are engaged in becoming. They, too, will make it necessary for us to engage in constant adjustments.

We will find parents, friends and lovers who will attempt to bind and distort us in their image, for their own convenience and comfort and usually in the name of love. We will discover society forcing us to conform to its needs, and attempting to squeeze us into its narrow mold. We will realize that education is most often filling us with irrelevant knowledge, teaching us what to learn, rather than how to use what we learn. We will become aware of institutions that are attempting to brainwash us and fill us with fear, guilt and shame. It is no surprise, then, that we proclaim defensively of the impossibility of becoming ourselves, "because 'they' will not allow us to do so."

It becomes clear why the philosopher-playwright, Jean Paul Sartre, in his short masterpiece, *No Exit*, concluded strongly that "Hell is other people."

This belief in our helplessness is further reinforced when we are asked to consider the history of personkind — the values, technology, religious beliefs and political systems. The results of this study produce a sad picture of ourselves as rigid, self-centered, impotent and frightened victims at the mercy of forces greater than we.

Our past has brought about unbelievable scientific discoveries which have extended us into the freedom of space. Still, on earth, we have riots in the streets and require formal legislation to assure the human being a basic livelihood and the right to live in dignity — the most basic of needs for the realization of our full humanness.

We live in a political system which prides itself on its sophisticated attitude and dedication to universal peace and freedom; but, we are faced with a past which reveals that we are no more peaceful, nonprejudicial or nonmilitant than the political systems we fear and condemn. We, too, have played an active part in the bloodiest century in recorded history. The study of recent religious history has produced no more optimistic or successful conclusions. We find a vast number of individuals who have felt abandoned and alienated from God and their churches and masses of misled zealots who have succeeded in rationalizing apathy, hate, prejudice, fear, violence and even mass murder as being the will of God!

From this dismal historic perspective of human beings and the institutions they have created, it is not surprising that we should look to agents outside ourselves to find any hope in the future. We are told that we have failed and that we shall continue to fail. Some philosophers and scientists even warn us of impending extinction. We are assured that at best we are "sick" and helpless and in great need of help. We are forced into a medical model of behavior which implies that our failure to fully function as human beings is due to "pathology" from which we must be "cured." We are characterized as being on a treadmill, moving in circles, going nowhere.

If we accept this picture of the person, it is questionable that we will ever gain the strength to reconstruct the emotional, physical and ecological wastes we have created. It is unlikely that we can ever restore a belief in human dignity. It seems rather more probable that we will not be able to avoid our own apocalypse.

I fully believe that we now have sufficient knowledge and understanding of the potential of personhood to make hatred, fear, pain, hunger, war and hopelessness obsolete. It is my contention that there is no looking back. We are not prisoners of the past. We can start where we are. We are enough. There are no "others" to blame — each of us *is* the other. If we look carefully at behavior, we usually discover that the emotional impotence, apathy, and the lack of understanding and resistance to change we see in others is really our own. We are they. We create our own private trap and are blind to the fact that it is of our own making.

When things are not done, it is we who have not done them; when there is misunderstanding, it is also ours; when we are in a state of emotional pain or tension, it is we who have chosen to be there. If we are not becoming all that we are, it is we who are not changing, and why we, therefore, must suffer our own non-being.

No "they" can teach or change us, only we can do that. No "they" can bring us peace or joy; these feelings are uniquely ours. (The world of fear, joy or tears is a very private and personal world.) No "they" can actualize us. Only we can accept the challenge of being our fully human selves. Only we can embrace ourselves and start anew. Only we can decide that we desire to live in full humanity.

The knowledge, that we make our own life, is not new, still most of us will resist it for if we were to accept it, we might be forced to change. We might have to face the pain and emptiness which arises from the knowledge of the unrealized self. We might have to assume the frightening, uncertain and demanding search for its actualization. We may finally have to cease blaming others and take upon ourselves the full responsibility for creating our own lives. There is no doubt that it is much easier to accept ourselves as we have been portrayed — helpless, hopeless, frightened failures, impotent to realize our actualization needs.

When we are born, we are almost all unrealized potential, and a thousand new possibilities are present in each of us. We can choose to be born again at any time and accept the challenge of the selves we have yet to meet, for the same is still true.

The world, too, is mostly unactualized potential, waiting upon us for its realization. The responsibility then, is ours. The manifestation of every person and the world in which we live is the minimum requirement of our existence, its major purpose and its only hope. The negligence of any of us to become a fully functioning part of the whole, no matter who we are or where we may be, will be potential which will be forever lost. We are of value to the degree to which we are constantly actualizing as the unique persons we are at each moment of our life. This goal may seem to be unattainable and unrealistic — a romantic ideal. Actualizing an ideal can be frustrating for it means we are mainly dealing with something imperceptible, an illusion. We are told the only hope lies in our taking an illusionary voyage toward some mystical, unrealized self. We have no assurance of where the trip will take us or what we will find when we get there. We are convinced that our present adjustment is at least an adjustment and to change would be an insecure risk at best. We are reminded that illusion is child's play and to follow illusion, naivete.

The manifestation of every person and the world in which we live is the minimum requirement of our existence, its major purpose and its only hope.

But it is an interesting phenomenon that the unrealized self demands visibility! It cannot be ignored for very long. It forces us either to move forward or backward or to live in confusion, anxiety and frustration. We are aware that there is something missing and we have a desperate need to discover what it is. We are driven toward growth in spite of the fact that, at best, the rewards are fogged in illusion; that we always seem ill-prepared; that we have failed so often in the past; that intellect misleads us; that emotions confuse us and that other travelers continuously interfere.

We find we have little to guide us in our search and must put our trust in the only power we have, that natural instinct that propels us toward creation, choice, liberation and change. We must yield to the challenge of becoming fully human and trust in our human processes in the hope that they will lead us there.

Elie Wiesel tells us of a rabbi who has said that when we cease to live and go before our Creator the question asked of us will not be why we did not become a messiah, a famous leader or to answer the great mysteries of life. The question will be simply — why did you not become you, the fully active, realized person that only you had the potential of becoming?

Our challenge then is clear — to make as much of the illusion as possible a reality. After all, our present reality is no more than what was once our illusions.

Where do we start? We start at the present moment. We abandon the past and embrace the now. We start, with the most valued possession and the only possession which can lead us to our own personal full humanity. We take the wise advise of Wiesel's rabbi, "We start with ourselves"!

THE STAGES OF GROWTH TOWARD FULL HUMANNESS

At first the infant,
Mewling and puking in the nurse's arms;
Then the whining school boy, with his satchel
And shining morning face, creeping like snail
Unwillingly to school. And then the lover,
Sighing like furnace, with a woeful ballad
Made to his mistress' eyebrow. Then a soldier,
Full of strange oaths, and bearded like the bard,
Jealous in honour, sudden and quick in quarrel,
Seeking the bubble reputation
Even in the cannon's mouth. And then the justice,
In fair round belly and good capon lin'd,
With eyes severe, and beard of formal cut,
Full of wise saws and modern instances;
And so he plays his part. The sixth age shifts
Into the lean and slippered pantaloon,
With spectacles on nose and pouch on side,
His youthful hose, well sav'd a world too wide
For his shrunk shank; and his manly voice,
Turning again toward childish treble, pipes
And whistles in his sound. Last scene of all,
That ends this strange eventful history,
Is second childishness and mere oblivion;
Sans teeth, sans eyes, sans taste, sans everything.

Shakespeare
As You Like It

CHAPTER 2

Jacques' view of the stage of life in Shakespeare's *As You Like It* is rather venomous and malicious, but very much in keeping with his charming, ill-natured character. Of course, we must admit to more than a little truth in what he says. However, there are other ways to look at the stages of human life. The physiologist may study them in terms of physical maturation and growth; the psychologist, in terms of personality development; the neurologist, in terms of motor functioning, and so on.

In this chapter, we will concern ourselves with the stages involved in growth and potentiality toward achieving full humanness. Growth toward full humanness will be seen to involve five fairly consistent, well-defined stages. These stages are hierarchical in nature; that is, each follows the other developmentally in a definite sequence. Yet each stage may be viewed as autonomous, complete and distinctive in itself and independent of each preceding one. Each stage has its own possibility for actualization, but one need not fully actualize one stage in order to move on to the next. For instance, we need not have a fully actualized childhood in order to become a fully active person in maturity. Each stage is characterized by responses and behaviors which appear to be more or less consistent in all human beings and serve to fulfill certain specific functions toward the actualization of that specific stage. In addition, these responses and behaviors facilitate the smooth passage to the following stage.

In other words, each stage has its own natural programming for continual growth. When we have reached a certain level of development in one period of life, we begin to experience illuminations, certain awarenesses which will serve to propel us to a higher vista. At this new height, we are able to perceive a fresh, undiscovered world. We are stimulated to become cognizant of it and to assimilate the complex and sophisticated data it offers. Each such new encounter will further aid us in extrapolating, refining and growing in humanness at each stage of life.

At first, this flash of illumination or variation in experiencing is generally ignored. What we see is not a part of our reality. But once brought into consciousness, the new insight repeatedly recurs, creating in us an anxiety which will prepare us and eventually compel us to accommodate and accept the new data. We will then begin to act out the actions and responses of our new stage. We participate actively in our new stage, and in so doing, master it and make it our own.

A good illustration of this phenomenon can be seen in the development of language in a newborn infant. Let us call our subject, Ted. At birth, Ted has no idea what language is, or indeed, that it even exists. He is born into a meaningless, noise-filled environment. His first natural language function is to babble spontaneously. He is, of course, totally unaware that it is by means of this babbling that the complex language functions known as thought and communication will occur. When he has reached a certain level of babbling, usually at about six months of age, he becomes maturationally ready to begin to listen to the sounds he utters. He listens to his sound and becomes consciously aware of it. At a certain level of continued awareness, he begins to repeat it with continued curious attention. He has now entered into the second stage of language development, echolalia. He will require many months of growth in awareness in echolalia prior to reaching the point of maturity, perhaps around the first year of life when he becomes aware of words. In this manner, all things being equal, he will become ready for, and master, in the proper hierarchical order, the subsequent stages of words, morphology, simple and complex syntax. He will have acquired language.

Further language acquisition will, of course, continue throughout his lifetime. He can engage in a continual polishing of the process which he had mostly mastered before he was three or four years of age. He will acquire new vocabulary, more subtle and lucid syntax, and new methods of problem solving and thinking.

This phenomenon is clearly paralleled in the dynamics of growing as a human person. If we squint at life, it appears to be a smooth process from birth to death, but if we look more closely, we can clearly see that the seemingly smooth continuum was actually neither smooth nor continuous, rather traumatic and broken by distinct and often violent periods. We began as curious infants absolutely dependent on other human beings for our very lives. In childhood, we tumbled clumsily over our mysterious surroundings to attempt to examine and discover the wonder of our vast new world. In adolescence, we fought for the choice to either emerge as a copy of everyone else, or to invent a new person and thus orchestrate our own personal destinies. Hopefully, having made the latter decision, we moved into adulthood

In a very real sense, then, each stage toward maturity is complete in itself and can be actualized independently of every other stage, but since we are programmed toward full Personhood, life is always both an active state of being, and an ever-changing state of becoming.

where we had to come to terms with our constantly growing selves and our places in an ever-changing universe. Somewhat secure in our dynamically emerging selves, we became ready for intimacy and coupling, meeting the need to overcome aloneness by forming a deep meaningful relationship with another. We decided to do this even at the price of relinquishing some of our selves in the process. We, at last, reach old age, the final stage to be actualized before life, as we know it, ceases.

Thus the major stages of growing toward full humanness: Infancy, Childhood, Adolescence, Maturity, Intimacy, and Old Age.

In a very real sense, then, each stage toward maturity is complete in itself and can be actualized independently of every other stage, but since we are programmed toward *full* Personhood, life is always both an active state of being, and an ever-changing state of becoming. It is a continual process of creating ourselves to meet the demands of the present and those of the future.

In the biological sciences, a similar phenomenon is referred to as epigenesis. It is the process by which development occurs as a gradual diversification and differentiation of an initially undifferentiated totality. Eric Linneberg describes it as follows:

Maturation may be characterized as a sequence of states. At each state, the growing organism is capable of accepting some specific input; this breaks down and resynthesizes in such a way that it makes itself develop into a new state. This new state makes the organism sensitive to new and different types of input, whose acceptance transforms it to yet a further state, which opens the way to still different input and so on. It is the story of embryological development observable in the formation of the body, as well as in certain aspects of behavior. Every stage of maturation is unstable. It is prone to change into specific directions but requires a trigger from the environment.[3]

The psychologist, Eric Erickson, has traced the major conflicts and resolutions in human personality development from infancy to old age using this theory. He hypothesized an epigenetic theory of growth in personality. He stated that there was a general ground plan for personality development and that out of this, parts arose, "each part having its time of special ascendency, until all parts have arisen to form the functioning whole." He described these parts as general stages where during critical periods of development, certain ego traits emerged. All stages, Erickson felt, existed in some form in the beginning, but each had its own critical period of development through a series of interrelated growth periods.

Abraham Maslow, of whom I have written earlier, was the pioneer in the study of growth in self-actualization and the fully functioning human person. He isolated and studied a type of lifetime human drive which seemed to propel the person toward growing as a fully functioning person. He found that through all stages of life a strong force moved human beings forward toward a unity of personality, to become a fuller being. He concluded that,

> Man demonstrates *in his own nature* a pressure toward fuller and fuller Being, more and more perfect actualization of his humanness in exactly the same naturalistic scientific sense that an acorn may be said to be 'pressing toward' being an oak tree, or that a tiger can be observed to 'push toward' being tigerish, or a horse toward being equine. Man is ultimately *not* molded or shaped into humanness or taught to be human. The role of the environment is ultimately to permit him or help him to actualize *his own* potentialities, not *its* potentialities. The environment does not give him potentialities and capabilities; he *has* them in inchoate or embryonic form, just exactly as he has embryonic arms and legs. And creativeness, spontaneity, self-hood, authenticity, caring for others, being able to love, yearning for truth are embryonic potentialities belonging to his species membership just as much as his arms and legs and brain and eyes.[1]

Maslow's major interest became this exploration and development of the unique, fully-realized human being. The subjects he selected for study were generally older people who had already gone through most of the stages of life and were visibly successful in the process of living as mature human beings. He studied self-actualization mainly as an end state. Certainly, there is wonder in the observation and study of persons who have come into old age having, to a large extent, realized their personhood. We have all known such people, individuals who live, as Maslow described, with a more efficient perception of reality, more openness, wholeness, spontaneity, a more firm identity, more objectivity, creativity, a more democratic outlook as well as a greater ability to love.

For me, living fully in each stage of life is the real challenge. It lies in the possibility of living our lives and actualizing ourselves at every moment, by living each moment and realizing its own completeness. The world has a different appearance, and therefore a different meaning and purpose at each moment of life. It is apparent, for instance, that the love one learns in childhood is radically different and has little relationship to that experienced by the mature person. So it is with dependence, loyalty, morality, and responsibility.

Each stage encompasses its own unique implications, requirements and potentials. These can only be actualized if each stage is lived and realized fully.

The question becomes, then, not only what does it mean to be a fully functioning mature adult, but more specifically, what constitutes a fully functioning child, adolescent, adult, lover, and old person.

The implications and discussion of these questions is the purpose of the remainder of this chapter.

Stage I. The Fully Functioning Infant and Child

Your children are not your children.
They are the sons and daughters of Life's longing for itself.
They come through you but not from you,
And though they are with you yet they belong not to you.
You may give them your love but not your thoughts,
For they have their own thoughts.
You may house their bodies but not their souls,
For their souls dwell in the house of tomorrow, which you cannot
visit, not even in your dreams.
You may strive to be like them, but seek not to make them like you.
For life goes not backward nor tarries with yesterday.

Kahil Gibran
The Prophet

The human infant and child are more helpless and dependent for a much longer period of time than any other living thing. Children and infants are, out of necessity, "natural slaves." Their identity in the world is being created by outside forces. They have no choice and because of their dependent state, receive all input from those people and things in their immediate life space. What food, warmth, nurturing, aural, visual and oral stimulation they will receive will be given by their parents and the specific society into which they are born.

Therefore, basic to actualization of the infant and child is what David Norton calls "responsible authority." Illustrating this expertly, he says,

> The dependence of childhood is a provisional dependence, and it is this provisionality that lends normative qualification to the authority that is exercised over children. Because that authority is trusted, it must make itself trustworthy. Because it is required to function unquestioned, it must be (for the child) unquestionable. And because childhood's dependence is provisional, the authority over it must be provisional authority, containing from the first, the anticipation of its own demise.[4]

The first requirement for the actualization of infants and children lies outside of their control and in the hands of responsible authority. This requires that the authority recognize and meet the basic physical, psychological and learning needs of the child. These authorities must, for awhile at least, assume the awesome responsibility for the lives of their children whose existence, at this point, is dependent upon them.

Infants and young children, though fresh and enthusiastic in their approach to life, have no autonomy and few tools for its creation. To organize their world and to interact in it, they will require a symbol system — language, common signs — which will help them to give structure to an otherwise chaotic environment. It is to be noted that each symbol children receive will not be their own, but will have been previously interpreted, identified and securely fastened to the world as perceived by other human beings. These authoritative figures will write a dictionary for their children and define the terms, cognitively, as well as affectively. They will suggest how their children should think and feel about the world. In spite of themselves, they will usually teach, in this way, their own lifestyles, fears, prejudices, anxieties and frustrations, along with their joys, hopes and desires for actualization. There is nothing wrong with this. It is a natural means for passing on the social and cultural mores and folkways necessary for continual survival and growth.

Therefore, for eventual autonomy, one of our major functions in all other stages of life will be to, what Norton calls, "disambiguate" the meaning of common terms, before we can call the world they symbolize our own.

However, infancy and childhood does not necessarily connote passivity. Children are also spontaneous actors, differentiators, assimilators, and accommodators. They are constantly discovering, learning, and are doing this more quickly and efficiently than they will at any other stage of their lives.

Childhood is a time for play, for experimentation, for fantasy, for exploration. Everything is new. Everything is curious. Few of us have been able to escape the fascination (and frustration) of watching a child explore. No place is too perilous, no object too valuable, no obstacle too insurmountable. They braille their way fearlessly over the world seeing, listening, responding. *The mystery the child is searching for, is itself.* The key to the mystery lies in the child's receptiveness. If its search is impeded or blocked, the child will scream in frustration. A child's nature requires experience, organiza-

Childhood is a time for play, for experimentation, for fantasy, for exploration. Everything is curious. Few of us have been able to escape the fascination (and frustration) of watching a child explore. No place is too perilous, no object too valuable, no obstacle too insurmountable. They braille their way fearlessly over the world seeing, listening, responding. The mystery the child is searching for, is itself.

tion, verification, and validation. All the material which is so essential for children to emerge as the fully functioning, unique individuals they are is already present in them. But in childhood, there is yet no personhood. Children are total potential. Even when basic expression is mastered, children are still mainly a copy of the others in their lives. Yet already in the specialness of their receptivity and environment, their unique selves are being formed.

Actualizing children may be seen, then, as mainly the task of responsible authorities. These individuals must understand the child's needs, respect the child's worth, and recognize their own vital and delicate role in verifying the child's eventual emerging self. They must permit the spontaneous activity, the awareness, evaluation and continual learning process if the child is to gain true control over its environment. The most damaging course of action is attempting to keep children from experience or protect them from pain, for it is at this time that children learn that life is a magic thing, if "not a rose garden." The parent's role is primarily to stand by with a goodly supply of bandaids.

Though childhood is a separate stage which can be completed and actualized in itself, it will afford us much valuable learning which can enrich our future life. For example, we shall want to maintain the childhood thirst for knowledge and exploration. We shall need to retain some of childhood's sense of wonder, of risk, of trust, of spontaneity, of fantasy. We shall want to discard childhood ways, essential to a child but destructive to an adolescent and adult, without losing the optimistic and zestful childlike view of life.

Stage II. The Fully Functioning Adolescent

Biff: "I just can't take hold, Mom, I can't take hold of some kind of life."

Arthur Miller
Death of a Salesman

It happened that green and crazy summer when Frankie was twelve years old. This was the summer when for a long time she had not been a member. She belonged to no club and was a member of nothing in the world. Frankie had become an unjointed person who hung around doorways and was afraid.

Carson McCullers
Member of the Wedding

Of all the stages of life, perhaps that one which we most remember is adolescence, for there seems to be no stage more filled with heartbreak, conflict and misunderstanding. We can remember the mixed hurt and delight. We retain the memory of how misunderstood we were, how mutable we were, how much we craved acceptance, and how desperately alone we felt. We wonder how it all began and where, along the line, we finally managed to survive and resolve the stage, if indeed we ever did.

Childhood was a time of "active dependence" when we were at the mercy of others. But also in childhood we became aware of our dependence and struggled to free ourselves even though we did not fully realize from or to what. We unconsciously became aware that, to use Norton's words, we had been "misidentified," that we were not slaves, that we were persons like the "others" in our lives — not merely "derivations." We became determined to discover ourselves.

It was at this point that we built the bridge between childhood and adolescence. But even our fully actualized childhood had ill prepared us for adolescence. This new stage was totally unique in its values, its obligations, and its virtues. It demanded a new, more aggressive mode of life in which what we had learned in childhood played a much lesser part.

Since as a child we had no real identity, we came to adolescence with neither the "I" to fall back on, nor the choices which were integral to it. We entered the stage of adolescence viewing life as overflowing with possibilities, only to discover that those possibilities were actually quite limited in access and so often frustrating. In assuming the struggle for "I," we were not only a problem for others, but also became a serious problem to ourselves. Since our responsible authorities had always spoken for us, we had little equipment for and experience in speaking for ourselves. We had to discover new and more personal symbols. This stage required our first and last act of release from the dependency of childhood. Therefore, we needed new input. Out of necessity, we had to extend ourselves further into our new and frightening world.

Like most trial-and-error experiences, we had to assume a more defensive attitude, a mode of life that would be more self-assertive. We had to be willing to take new risks and engage in experimentation with little concern for the consequences. We had to participate in extremes of behavior, be aggressive, even insolent, to find our way. We found ourselves engaging in passionate commitments which we abandoned as quickly and abruptly as they had been assumed.

It is no wonder that going through adolescence is considered one of development's most herculean tasks. It is also a task of paramount importance, for its main purpose is to develop and come to terms, for the first time, with one's unique person. It is the initial realization that we are not *they*, but *we, ourselves,* and I. The pity is that the most vital characteristics of adolescence, so necessary for realization of the self, are those most abhorred by adults and society, and, therefore, most often frustrated.

It is not surprising that one of the main problems in adolescence is one of being misconceived, misinterpreted and misjudged by everyone. We feel banished, estranged and alone. The others in our life do not comprehend that our behavior, our inconsistencies, our insolence, our resentment, our snap judgments, are not to be taken personally. They are merely our new-found way of probing and exploring our potentialities. We cannot, as yet, make definite choices for we are not even sure of who we are or what alternatives are available to us. Every indefinite action, every questionable judgment, every incongruity is our way of coming to terms with the denuding and unfolding of self.

Psychologists and educators for years have been mystified by the adolescent's clannishness. They have seen this as the adolescent's way of seeking identity as part of a group. If they were to look more deeply, they would perhaps discover, as Norton suggests, the superficiality of their observation. In actuality, adolescents feel more dissociated and isolated than they will at any other stage of their lives. The togetherness they seem to seek is merely, what Norton calls, "a cloak drawn over a profound and fully aware solitude." It is a selective way to hide so that their individuation will not be revealed until they are more secure in its reality.

In fact, this personal disjunction is perhaps the major force toward actualizing adolescents. In this solitude, they will find the space to explore, to experience, and to attempt to make so many of their important life choices. They will have to choose their work, make decisions regarding marriage and children, and select options of lifestyle. They will be required to explore among the hundreds of options available and to accept and discard them in terms of these personal needs if the desire to break away from home and parents and to become separate persons is to be fulfilled.

This is the major requirement of adolescence. It is a time for introspection, for trial and error, for developing sufficient autonomy to arrive at those judgments which will determine the first concept of self.

It is apparent that the fully functioning adolescent is not too attractive to the adult world, for he or she will be involved mostly in misinterpreted, "obnoxious" behavior, but behavior which is absolutely necessary for survival as a person. This behavior, happily, is passing behavior. But it must be permitted if adolescents are to begin to emerge as individuals, embrace their unique selves as their own, and pass into the stage of maturity with their new-found identity securely in hand.

Stage III. The Fully Functioning Mature Person

The adult with a capacity for true maturity is one who has grown out of childhood without losing childhood's best traits. He has retained the basic emotional strengths of infancy, the stubborn autonomy of totterhood, the capacity for wonder and pleasure and playfulness of the preschool years, the capacity for affiliation and the intellectual curiosity of the school years, the idealism and passion of adolescence. He has incorporated these into a new pattern of development dominated by adult stability, wisdom, knowledge, sensitivity to other people, responsibility, strength, and purposiveness.

Joseph Stone and Joseph Church
Childhood and Adolescence

Maturity is both a static and a dynamic concept. It is static in the sense of its being a definite and separate stage in itself, emerging from the complexities, searchings and revelations of childhood and adolescence. It implies, as is indicated in its Latin root, a state of being ripe, of full growth and development, a state of completion. But unlike the previous stages of childhood and adolescence through which we have passed and abandoned, our maturity will be forever developing and can only be defined by the degree and quality of its presence throughout future times of our lives. It is like the concepts of love or knowledge — there can never be an end to acquiring either, only an intense aspiration for

41

experiencing more of both. It is, therefore, a concept of both being and becoming.

With maturity we have finally acquired an *I*, a *self*, a *center* which, though not fully realized, we can accept as a start. We recognize its dynamic nature, its debt to the past, but accept the fact that its future realization is independent from that past, that our life is not merely an epilogue to what has already happened. We choose ourselves in the present. We accept the future as our challenge, not in the sense of waiting for it, but living the now in a way so as to make it happen in the most lively way. We accept our newlyfound *I* as an everchanging concept because we know that without such a forceful, potent and constantly changing phenomenon, interacting in a limitless environment can never know full realization.

Carl Rogers[5] is perhaps one of the leading exponents of this dynamic approach to maturity. He feels that the adult good life is more than just a fixed state of reduced tension or a homeostatic condition to be aspired to and in which one can be comfortable functioning in a complex society. He sees maturity not as an actualization or a state of fulfillment, but rather as a process which is forever changing and developing.

There are many theories of what constitutes a mature human person. These theories are only meaningful if studied through a context which includes unique cultural, ethical, behavioral and historical considerations. Freud and Erickson, for example, may be said to have seen growth to maturity as a resolution of the conflict created by the person on the one hand, and society on the other. Maturity for them involved a dynamic ego balance of these two forces, one inside, which they called the Id, and one outside, which they labeled the Super Ego.

On the other hand, such theorists as Rank, May and Bakan, though they agree with a basic conflict model, see the forces of conflict to be totally within the person, with maturity being achieved through a dynamic balance intrapsychically, a resolution of these conflicts within themselves.

Other major models of maturity were created by Rogers and Maslow who saw it as a continual process toward actualization, with the forces to realize one's inherent maturational potentials being totally within the individual. Adler, Allport and Fromm though agreeing essentially with the theory of fulfillment, saw the process as one of achieving perfection by means of internalizing and living up to certain culturally defined ideas of excellence and meaningfulness.

Kelly, Maddi, and Fiske saw a consistency model with maturity (though they do not name it as such) being essentially the ability to maintain a balance between one's expectations and the feedback which comes from one's chosen environment. Here the key was in the person's ability to decrease any inconsistencies between the self and environmental feedback. If this was done, the person became quiescent and comfortable, i.e., mature.

Except for the consistency model, all the theories of maturity offer suggestions as to the characteristic attitudes and actions of the mature person. Although there are some conflicts among the theorists as to what actually constitutes

---

Maturity is not a goal, but rather a process.

full maturity, there are also several essential commonalities.

It is generally agreed that mature persons have a sense of ego identity, a sense of the "I" mentioned above, a sense of who they are, separate and apart from the others in their life. But these separate persons also realize the need for both physical and psychological intimacy — a need to relate on a deep, meaningful level with others.

Mature persons have a sincere desire to be productive and to give of that production to others. They desire to create and share their creations. They accept their lives and work with satisfaction and joy. They live life as, in Otto Rank's terms, an "artist" (not necessarily an artist who writes or paints, but more an artist of life). They put their talents into each endeavor and their imagination into recreating their lives each day. The mature artists of life are spontaneous, accepting, flexible, receptive to new experience, suspicious of reality. They are harmonious with external forces, but autonomous, busy with the processes of inventing their own lives. They see existence as a series of choices, the selection of which they must determine, and for which they are singularly responsible. They care about, respect and appreciate the world and society in which they live and the others who cohabit it, even though they may not wholly agree with them. They believe in their own personal needs and potentialities and realize that these may often conflict with those of others, but they recognize that conflict can be a positive force for growth and change.

Mature persons have a deep spiritual sense in terms of their relationship with nature and other persons, and recognize the continual wonder of life and living. They make full use of their potentialities, accept themselves as part of the greater mystery of life, and share their love, joy and wisdom in an open, nonexploitative, responsible fashion.

In essence, then, fully functioning mature human persons are continually growing, for they realize that maturity is not a goal, but rather a process; that the essence of maturity lies in creative and responsible choices. They have a flexible but nonconformist sense of identity, an accepting and vivid sense of who they are, what they can be and where their powers lie.

Fundamental to the mature person is the ability to form deep, intimate, meaningful relationships which are based upon an "unconditional regard" for the uniqueness of others. They are affectionate, loving and sexually responsive; they are sociable, have friends and a sense of community. They are productive workers and dedicated to their labors. They embrace change for the improvement of themselves and others, as well as of the society in which they live. They are self-determined, inventive, good-humored, and comforatble in their world, with themselves and with others.

Stage IV. The Fully Functioning Intimate Person

The Buddhas and the Christs are born complete. They neither seek love nor give love, because they are love itself. But we who are born again and again must discover the meaning of love, must learn to live love as the flower lives beauty.

Henry Miller
Insomnia

Since intimacy is basically an ability and interest in relating closely in both the physical and psychological sense to others, and is inherent, to some degree, in all the aforementioned stages, many will find it strange that it should be included here as a unique and separate stage.

The stages of life so far have taken us to the point of dealing with the emergence and acceptance of the unique self, the *I* which will grant us our identities and accord meaning to our lives. Until this time, we were mainly at the mercy of others. To survive, we were forced to accept their reality, values and lifestyles as our own. We spoke their words and moved at their behest. We found ourselves faced with the struggle which William Blake realized in his poem,

I must create a System or be enslav'd by another
Man's.
I will not Reason and Compare: My business
is to Create.

True intimacy is a positive force only if it is a combining of strengths and energies with other mature persons for the continued growth of each.

With this decision, we have reached our early maturity and have accepted the responsibility for declaring and creating a new, heretofore not present, person. We have agreed to engage in a commitment to self.

Intrinsic in this commitment are certain natural conflicts. If we wish to free ourselves from enslavement, we must choose freedom and the responsibility this entails. If we do not wish to feel dependence, we must select independence, and accept those conflicts which are inherent in the choice. If we want to overcome loneliness, then we must embrace intimacy, with all the ramifications this choice suggests.

Of all of these, it is the latter choice which seems to create the greatest conflict. Both Rollo May and Eric Erickson stress the import of the intimacy versus isolation adjustment.

Isolation is a frightening concept for most individuals. We have a strong need for togetherness, for supporting relationships. We have a powerful, natural drive toward sensual and sexual gratification. We need nurturing, assistance, encouragement, affection and love. We are faced, then, with the cardinal choice, either to be intimate, which will require some relinquishing and readjusting of the newly-valued autonomous self, or to be isolated. The latter choice is devastating and threatening, and perhaps forces upon us one of the single most vital decisions of maturity. Most individuals will choose intimacy at any cost — for their alternative lies in loneliness.

We will always need others for our own continued growth and validation. True intimacy is a positive force only if it is a combining of strengths and energies with other mature persons for the continued growth of each. It must be a willful relinquishing of some aspects of each person's autonomous self in the desire to *get more*. It is mainly through intimate, continuing companionships that we can be presented with another's unique world and can receive an honest reflection of our own. It is for this reason that it is so easy to *love* casual friends, and so difficult to *love* a lover. Our investment in a friend is far less revealing and demanding than that for a lover, but also, in the long run, far less rewarding in its compensation toward growth.

Differing degrees of intimacy may be found in a variety of relationships at the onset, satisfying diverse intimacy needs, from casual social and sexual relationships to deep and prolonged friendships and attempts at forming a permanent union such as marriage. Casual relationships and friendships can provide the individual with opportunities for brief shared experiences, and the exchanging of information, feelings and ideas which can serve to counteract feelings of isolation and boredom. But studies have shown that only those intimate relationships which extend beyond sociability and offer opportunities for prolonged togetherness, such as cohabitation or marriage, can offer us the most growth-producing setting in which we may be ourselves and express that self freely within a reliable, safe, accepting, encouraging and trusting environment. They afford us the most vital opportunity to overcome loneliness, to undertake and explore the human experience without fear or distraction.

It is often said that the best indication of our maturity is in our ability to form growing, meaningful and lasting relationships. As Erich Fromm states, "Mature man finds himself and his roots only in creative relatedness to the world and the feeling of oneness with all men and nature."

Stage V. The Fully Functioning Old Person

*The afternoon of life must also have a significance of
its own and cannot be merely a pitiful appendage to life's
morning.*

Carl Jung

*Do not go gentle into that good night. Old age should
burn and rage at close of day.*

Dylan Thomas

*The tragedy of old age is not that one is old, but that
one is young.*

Oscar Wilde

Our present society attempts not only to take away our
right to death, but also our right to life. It often robs
childhood of joy, relegates the rebellious adolescent to an
empty cause, intimidates the adult to continual uncertainty,
but most tragic of all, denies us the dignity of our old age.

The aging are robbed of choices, the very thing for which
they have spent a lifetime of struggle to acquire, and without
choice, they are relegated to decay — alone, lonely and
helpless.

We are not allowed to get old without a deep sense of

shame. We are told that wrinkles are to be abhorred; that to lose one's physiological vigor is to make one useless; that with our senses dimmed we have lost all hope for joy, esthetics and productivity. We are influenced to hide our age, cover our wrinkles and dye our hair. Lest we become a burden, we are afforded special communities for the aged in which we are told we can find comfort and peace with others like ourselves.

The implications of all of this is that there is something not quite right about growing physically old. We ignore the fact that there is more to aging than chronological age. No matter the condition or vulnerability of the external body, the person it serves becomes no less a human being with human capacities for feelings, for sharing, for friendship, for creativity, for production.

It is certainly true that there are definite and obvious biological and physiological changes that occur with age; but the aged are still real people and will behave as such if allowed to do so. In fact, in most cases, the years have helped them to grow in honesty and acceptance. Senility seems to be the result more of feelings of uselessness and timelessness than of physical and mental decay.

Old age comes to most of us as a surprise. We seldom feel our age. It is rather a matter of its being reflected upon us by others than by our own awareness. We certainly become cognizant of the erosion of our physical endurance, but that is hardly reason for self-pity, self-indulgence, bigotry or retirement.

The challenge is to be true to each stage of life. Old age, too, has a purpose, and we must choose to either sacrifice or

The challenge is to be true to each stage of life.

actualize it. Hope is a real part of the future, and even in old age, one can choose hope — not hope for immortality or revived youth, not a hope for retreat into the past because one finds comfort there and there is no place else to go, but rather a continued search in each moment for the source of one's self. It becomes necessary to give meaning to the newly-initiated values, virtues and obligations which old age brings and the often more intense ways of feeling, sensing and experiencing it offers.

Maslow labeled this phase the "post-mortem life." He described it as a time when, "Everything gets doubly precious, gets piercingly important. You get stabbed by flowers and by babies and by beautiful things."

Death is no stranger to age since, in a very real sense, life is a matter of a series of deaths as each act or stage is completed. Montaigne has suggested that, in fact, "death is the moment when dying ends." True, death is simply a running out of borrowed time. But that, too, is not a new insight for the aged, for there has never, in any stage, been *enough* time. But time itself is meaningless when it contains the past and future in the present. The task of old persons is to continue to live the now.

Even when we decide that life, whether lived in wealth or poverty, in joy or despair, in pain or in comfort, has, in actuality, led us nowhere, we must choose to continue to live life and move forward. Unrealized life itself is purpose enough.

Death, too, is purposeful. It is not simply an end to life, but

If life's meaning is to be discovered, it is intrinsic in each stage as we assume the challenge of actualizing every moment of every day as we live it.

also, as Elizabeth Kubler-Ross designates, the last stage of growth.

Fully functioning old persons do not have time to sit back and wait for death. They are faced with the task of working through and actualizing two new stages — their old age, and their personal death. They must build confidence and give their limited time on earth purpose; they must make peace with the knowledge that someday they will be outgrown or even forgotten, but that the experience of life will have been enough. To ignore this task is to miss the opportunity for personal continued life in dignity through the pursuit of the experiences which only old age can offer. Their most precious treasures are still the continual surprises which daily living can bring. They can choose life. They need not choose confusion, fear, despair, loneliness and isolation. They can choose themselves as still unrealized potential and, in so doing, they can choose continued actualization.

The meaning of life is not to be found in looking back over this continuous strand from childhood to old age. Life is more than simply being born, growing up and maturing. If life's meaning is to be discovered, it is intrinsic in each stage as we assume the challenge of actualizing every moment of every day as we live it.

We have the basic tools necessary — our inborn potentials; our time of life and death....a life which is ours to be "outlived." The self that we are now contains the actualization potential which will fulfill us. The challenge is ours.

SOME VITAL VIEWS OF THE
FULLY FUNCTIONING PERSON

*Man has come to control all other forms of life because
he has taken more time in which to grow up; when he
takes still more time, and spends this time more wisely,
he may learn to control and remake himself.*

Will Durant
The Story of Philosophy

*The purpose of life, after all, is to live it, to taste
experience to the utmost, to reach out eagerly and
without fear for newer and richer experience.*

Eleanor Roosevelt

CHAPTER 3

We have been reaching out and puzzling for an under-standing of personkind for over 400 centuries, at least as far back as Neanderthal Man. We have been mystified by creatures like ourselves and overwhelmed by the complexi-ties and perplexities of their natures and the societies they created. We continuously strive to comprehend them with the hope that in this manner we can better understand and live in harmony with them and with ourselves.

We are astonished with the startling way in which human beings seem to have exploded forth in such a short period of time. We are bewildered when we consider that today's person has the same basic brain and body as his or her Ice Age relatives, but this same brain has evolved ideas, belief systems, habits and customs which have put us worlds apart.

Since the emergence of the first symbols drawn some 25 centuries ago on the wall of a dark cave somewhere in what is now Western Europe, we have discovered continual recorded evidence of the human person's growing curiosity regarding matters of the good life and day-to-day living.

Throughout history, ideas have emerged which have persisted and had an immense impact upon human beings, their ethics and their lifestyles. Many of these have evolved into formal philosophical and religious systems which have been adopted by millions as their *way* of life.

No attempt was made to consider all of these here, for this would be infeasible and require several volumes. Much is written on these philosophies and their ethics, and is available for the interested reader elsewhere. In addition, no attempt was made to be comprehensive in the brief characterizations of the social, religious and philosophical systems discussed here, for this would be inconceivable in terms of the vastness of the subject and my limited abilities and knowledge. (My amateur status as scholar of comparative philosophies and religions will soon be apparent.) It is also well beyond the scope and purpose of this work.

I have, therefore, chosen to be simplistically brief and selective. For this I feel certain that I shall be sorely criticized. To those whom I insult or irritate, I shall apologize in advance. But I shall risk the criticisms, for my purpose is devious but simple. I wish to illustrate that though we may differ greatly in how, who and what we worship, the basic code of behavior is common to all. It is this common denominator which binds us together in humanity and has helped us to continue to grow and survive. It will be used to serve as an historical view of the universality of the concept of the fully functioning human person.

The Way of Taoism

If name be needed, wonder names them both;
From wonder into wonder
Existence opens.

The Way of Life
Lao Tzu (Bynner Translation)

For over two thousand years a large number of the world's people have been highly influenced by a philosophy of great vitality, called Taoism.

Taoism was introduced in China during the Chinese Middle Kingdom, about the third or fourth century B.C., by a man called Lao Tzu in a short work of less than 6000 words, named The Tao (The Way). His philosophy was later expanded and interpreted by an ingenious philosopher and poet, Chuang Tzu, during the second half of the fourth century B.C.

The major aim of the Taoist philosophy is toward the internal integration and harmony of each person. As such, it is a way of nonconformity. It suggests that each of us can only achieve our personal full humanity through the process of unlearning what we have already learned so as to offer us the opportunity to return in harmony with all things as we were in the beginning.

Egotism is seen as being at the root of all disharmony and

thus the main causal factor of human suffering. For this reason, the person must strive to become egoless. With the loss of ego desires, one is also released of inner conflicts.

Lao Tzu suggested that fully functioning persons would therefore have few desires and be unattached to people and things. They would live in terms of their own self-estimation, not that of others. They would strive for natural simplicity and spontaneous living and rid themselves of artificiality and compulsion.

Fully functioning Taoists are not at the mercy of their emotions. They strive to perceive themselves accurately in terms of their observable strengths and weaknesses. They see themselves as unique and therefore in competition with no one. They practice "non-action." Nonaction to the Taoist is not a passive condition but rather a subtle form of action. The way of water is used as a common metaphor for this. In the words of Lao Tzu —

> As the soft yield of water cleaves the obstinate stone,
> So to yield with life solves the insoluable:
> To yield, I have learned, is to come back again.
> But this unworded lesson,
> This easy example,
> Is lost upon men.

Taoists see power in morality and are, therefore, sensitive to society and the feelings of others. They are nonjudgmental and attempt to respond to the attitude of others more than to their actions. They reject violence, oppression and power. They refuse to participate in the conquest of nature or in the exploitation of others. Rather, they strive to become the friendly coworker of both man and nature. Their goal is harmony with all things, permitting all things to work out their own destinies. The Taoist sees this as the ultimate in maturity.

Lao Tzu, and especially Chuang Tzu, emphasized that the fully functioning Taoist must be always engaged in self-transcendence. This is the process by which they are able to see all things in terms of not just self, but rather as an ultimate, undifferentiated wholeness. Pain and despair arise from a breaking with this wholeness. "The Way" to the good life is by means of the transcendence of all distinctions, differences and differentiations, for these merely serve to bring about fragmentation which causes weakness and impotence. They see the opposite of fragmentation as universal oneness, acceptance and love. At the heart of Taoist love is the ability to merge as a part of all things.

The fully functioning Taoists are convinced that natural right and goodness is innate. They, therefore, attempt to live their lives naturally and in such a manner as to encourage peace in conflict, unity in separation, love and transcendence in confusion and chaos.

The Way of Confucianism

As to the way — the intelligent man goes beyond
it, the imbecile does not go far enough.

—From The Chang Yong, 4

Confucius said:
....When a man carries out the principals of conscien-
tiousness and reciprocity he is not far from the
universal law. What you do not wish others
should do unto you, do not do unto them.

— From The Golden Mean of Tsesze XIII

Confucius was born in China around the time of the Buddha in India and Pythagoras in Greece, 552 B.C.

Like most of the truly great ethical and moral leaders, he wrote nothing. His teachings were recorded (by his disciples) into four major works a century after his death, and referred to as the Shu (the Four Classics). Of these, the major ethical work is felt to be the Luen Yu.

Confucius was a man, not a God. He expounded neither theoric nor universal dictum. He offered no formulas for humanity or divine commandments. He avoided dealing with mysticism and spiritual matters and concerned himself rather with the tangible, day-to-day activities, complexities and dilemmas of life.

He is often referred to as the greatest teacher in Chinese history and devoted his entire life to his humanistic teachings and to the training of moral character. In essence he may be said to have been more of a social reformer than a religious leader. His major concerns were with stimulating individuals toward having the courage to be themselves and gain the wisdom to be an active part of the society in which they lived. In fact, the purpose of all self-actualization, according to Confucius, was to help us discover our part in the process of ordering and harmonizing the world.

In Chapter V of *The Great Learning,* Confucius states,

> The ancients who wish to show their fine characters to the world would first bring order to their states. Those who wished to bring order to their states would first regulate their households. Those who wished to regulate their households would first cultivate their personhood.

He continues —

> Those who wished to cultivate their personhood would first achieve the rectification of their minds. Those who wished to achieve the rectification of their minds would first achieve the sincerity of their wills. Those who wished to achieve the sincerity of their wills would first extend their knowledge. The extension of knowledge depends on the investigation of things. When things are investigated, knowledge is extended; when knowledge is extended, the security of the will is achieved; when security of the will is achieved, the mind is rectified; when the mind is rectified, the personhood is cultivated.

In essence, for Confucionists, this points the way to full functioning in humanness. It suggests active investigation for the sake of knowledge; this knowledge is directed to strengthen the mind as well as the will and results in the continual cultivation of personhood and society. It develops "jen," perfect harmony, which is mainly concerned with growth in self-respect, magnanimity, good faith, loyalty, diligence and beneficence.

Personhood, for Confucius, was not a state of perfection but rather an ever-changing, very human state, often accompanied by anxiety. He said of himself "Not applying myself to the achievement of virtue, not explaining clearly to myself what I study, not accomplishing what I conceive to be my duty, not concerning myself with my own faults: These are my anxieties." (Luen Yu, VII, 3).

In an excellent book called *Confucius and Chinese Humanism*, (1969), the author, Pierre Du-Dinh, describes the person of Confucius in a most illuminating way. He suggests that since Confucius was exemplary of his idea of the fully functioning person it seems appropriate to relate his qualities. He states that "his manner was gentle, calm, austere and inspired respect without arousing fear. He was sober and serene and at the same time cordial and gay. He was respectful and given to acts of spontaneous sensitivity. He appeared both noble and humble. He had a sensible and accurate image of himself and devoted all of his energies to being what he wished to be." Exemplary, indeed!

Confucius' fully functioning persons would not only be concerned with self-cultivation and harmony but would be equally concerned with relationships with other human beings. They would feel deeply that a person could become fully human only as he or she was in union with another or others. The essence of this union would be love, for without love there could be no true personhood.

There is, therefore, no place for negligence, hypocrisy, dishonesty, deceitfulness, egoism or provincialism, for the goal of the fully functioning Confucionist is the unification of all things in the wedding of the polarities of self-giving and self-loving which they believe are one.

Full humanity, for the person, comes from one's striving for human cultivation and perfectability and applying this perfecting unification of self to others, the state and the world.

The Way of Buddhism

A wicked man who reproaches a virtuous one is like
one who looks up and spits at heaven; the spittle
soils not the heaven, but comes back and defiles
his own person.

Buddha
— The Sutra of Forty-Two Sections

There are two extremes, O bretheren, which a holy
man should avoid — the habitual practice of. . .self
indulgence, which is vulgar and profitless. . .and
the practice of self mortification, which is pain-
ful and equally profitless.

Buddha
— The sermon at Benares

The religious life, Malunkyapulta, does not depend
on the dogma that the world is eternal; nor does
the religious life, Malunkyapulta, depend on the
dogma that the world is not eternal. No matter what
the dogma. . .There still remains birth, old age,
death, sorrow, lamentation, misery, grief and despair.
And it is against these here on earth that I am
prescribing.

Buddha
— The Majjhima-Nikaya

The teachings of Buddhism arose from an unusually sensitive concern and inquisitiveness regarding human suffering. They were the thoughts of an Indian prince in the sixth century, Siddartha Gautama, who questioned the purpose of pain, sickness, old age and death. At 29 he set forth to grow in the experience, sensitivity and knowledge which would eventually lead him to an answer, to Buddhahood and the formation of an ethic which presently claims over 150 million adherents.

Modern Buddhism has taken basically three distinct forms: a more established form called Hanayana, a rather diffuse form called Mahayana and an esoteric form called Tantric Buddhism. Each claims a somewhat different interpretation of the Buddha's teachings, each reflecting the society or historic period in which it was formed. It is, therefore, triply difficult to draw many generalities which would accurately satisfy all schools. But commonalities in their ethics do exist. For example, it can safely be said that all the sects do attempt to achieve a resolution of human conflict by means of an internal integration of personality. The goal is to achieve harmony with the ultimate Oneness. This process may take several cycles of rebirth before one can achieve true transcendence as Buddha did. This formed the base of the Buddha's teaching.

The main concern in Buddhism, then, is with the person and the person's life on earth — with suffering and how to be rid of it. The Buddhist sees life as a dynamic becoming instead of a static being, and all things in life as being impermanent and in constant change, either being produced or deteriorating and dying. According to Buddhism, to hold on to what is impermanent results in suffering, but suffering can be suppressed. The method for suppressing suffering is by following the Eightfold Path, consisting of right view, right intention, right speech, right action, right livelihood, right effort, right mindfulness of the now and right concentration.

Conflict for the Buddhist arises from desire. It is desire which brings on greed, lust, hatred and attachment. It is necessary to transcend these desires for they are mainly the irrationality which obscures an accurate perception of reality. They also create dualities which separate subject and object and cause conflicts.

Transcending the self may be accomplished by conscientious right living of the Middle Path — a moderate, but comprehensive and practical system of ethics. It can also be achieved intuitively, spontaneously, all at once in direct confrontation.

For a fuller life the Buddhist stresses kindness, virtue, love, compassion, noninjury, liberality, moderation, temperance, the Golden Rule, and mutual duty in human relationships.

Fully functioning (growing) Buddhists are therefore moral, aware, constantly seeking knowledge, free of desire and expectation. They are more conceptual than emotional, though loving kindness and compassion are emphasized, as are such traits as honesty, compassion, respect, courtesy, hospitality, generosity and honoring the rights of others.

The Buddhist way is a solitary one, extremely individualistic and inner directed. It is self-authenticating. It needs no other validation.

The Way of Hinduism

Know the Self to be sitting in the Chariot, the body to be the chariot, the intellect the charioteer, and the mind the reins. The senses they call the horses, the objects of the senses their roads. When he is in union with the body, the senses, and the mind, then wise people call him the Enjoyer.

— The Upanishads, V

Depend not on another, but lean instead on thyself. . . .True happiness is born of self reliance. . . .

— The laws of Manu

Knowledge is the holiest of holies, the god of gods, and commands the respect of crowned heads: shorn of it a man is but an animal. The features and furniture of one's house may be stolen by thieves, but knowledge, the highest treasure, is above all stealing.

— The Puranas II

Hinduism is actually a multitude of religions, the oldest in the world, and has at least 230 million followers.

The sacred scriptures which make up the basis for modern Hinduistic ethics are to be found in several works but mainly in the Mahabharata and the Ramayana. The former contains the profound and beautiful *Bhagavad Gita*, the "Song of God."

Hinduism is one of the most human of religions. What it lacks in abstraction, inhibition and refinement it makes up for in humanism. Even their Gods often became humans and walked freely on earth among other men and women, living actively and with passion.

The essence of Hindu thought lies in the belief that sensory life is transitory and thus, meaningless. Individuals must live life in the universal sense. In finding salvation they can select either a contemplative life of inaction and meditation and knowledge or a life of selfless action, assuming day-to-day material duties and obligations.

Krishna, one of the Hindu Gods, gives the loving and inquisitive Arjina advice in the "Yoga of Devotion" from the *Bhagavad Gita.* He suggests the way that Arjina should live his life in humanness.He says,

A man should not hate any living creature. Let him be friendly and compassionate to all. He must free himself from delusion of "I" and "mine." He must accept pleasure and pain with an equal tranquility. He must be forgiving, even contented, self controlled....

He neither molests his fellow men, nor allows himself to become disturbed by the world. He is no longer swayed by joy and passion, anxiety and fear.

He does not desire or rejoice in what is pleasant. He does not dread what is unpleasant or grieve over it. He remains unmoved by good or evil fortune.

His attitude is the same toward friend or foe. He is indifferent to honor and insult, heat and cold, pleasure and pain. He is free from attachment. He values praise and blame equally. He can control his speech. He is content with whatever he gets. His home is everywhere and nowhere.

When he completes this discourse Krishna adds:

Now I have taught you that wisdom which is the secret of secrets. Ponder it carefully. Then act as you think best. These are the last words that I shall say to you, the deepest of all truths.

So ends the Bhagavad Gita!

The Pirranas, 18 books of "Ancient Love" also offer advice for living fully as a human person. Section II, called "Wise Counsel" suggests the following:

Avoid the company of the erudite miscontent. Sit in the assembly of the honest; combine with those that are good and virtuous.

The vile are ever prone to detect the faults of others, though they be as small as mustard seeds, and persistently shut their eyes against their own, though they be as large as Vilva fruits.

Liberty or emancipation is the only happiness vouch-safed to man.

True happiness lies in the extinction of all emotions.

Apprehension is where affection is. Renounce affection and you shall be happy.

A vast, deep and childlike faith in all, a universal clemency, and a close and watchful unveiling of his own god-like inherent virtues, are the traits which mark the noble soul.

As can be seen, fully functioning persons who live in Hindu wisdom possess a vast, flexible and assimilating ethic at the center of which is truth, goodness, and righteousness. The Mahabharata states:

This is the sum of all — righteousness.
In causing pleasure or in giving pain
In doing good or injury to others
A man obtains a proper rule of action
By looking at his neighbor as himself.

The Way of Islam

*There is no fault in those who believe and do deeds of
righteousness — God loves the good doers.*

The Koran

*Thou seest the evildoers going in fear of what they have
earned, that is about to fall on them; but those who
believe and do righteous deeds are in Meadows of the
Gardens.*

The Koran

*I do not ask of you a wage for this, except love for the
kinfolk; and whosoever gains a good deed, we shall give
him increase of good in respect of it.*

The Koran

Mohammedanism (Islam) is one of the world's youngest
religious philosophies and perhaps the most widespread,
commanding over 200 million people. It was founded in
Mecca by Mohammed (570-632 A.D.), an Arab who preached
that his teachings were based upon Divine revelations. These
teachings were later compiled in the *Koran*, the holy book of
Islam.

It is generally agreed that Mohammed was a true moral
reformer. He insisted that each person was responsible for
the manner in which he or she lived life for — "On the Day of
Judgment everyone shall be responsible for himself alone."

75

He promoted a universal brotherhood among the Arabs in which justice and charity were to be paramount.

He was quite definite about the human virtues to be practiced as well as the evils to be avoided.

Among the highest of virtues is almsgiving. Equally important and related to this are hospitality, kindness, respect, and a deep feeling of community. No matter how scattered and far removed the Muslim people are, there is only one Islamic community. This community accepts only one absolute God and accepts with compassion the humanness of persons who are attempting to be one with Him and the nature of the world in which they must make their way.

In the Islamic tradition it is a privilege for persons to participate in the human state, for this allows them the possibility of fulfilling God's Plan. "Lo," says the Koran (XXXIII; 72), "we offered the trust unto the heavens and the earth and the hills, but they shrank from hearing it and were afraid of it. And man assumed it." Therein lies the significance, grandeur and seriousness of the human condition for the Muslim.

The Koran contains mainly three types of messages for living as a person — a doctrinal message which deals with the human being's place in the structure of reality, a metaphysical message about the nature of the Absolute and a doctrinal message about human life, existence and its meaning. This latter aspect deals in detail with all the teaching necessary for their followers to understand who they are, where they are, where they are going, and how they are to get there.

Though Muslims, as humans, love this world and are

deeply attached to it, they know that through a proper life and the Koran they can find the peace, harmony and unity essential to discard their worldly attachment and become one with God. It is mainly through the studying and reading of the Koran that the person is offered a practical guide to living and the knowledge necessary to transcend it.

To understand the full meaning of the fully functioning person in Islam it is often recommended that one study the life of the Prophet Mohammed, for he represents not only their spiritual being but a leader of men. It is to be remembered, too, that Mohammed never claimed to be a God — but rather His prophet — and as such was a man among men. He is referred to as the "most noble of all creation."

From the Muslim point of view then, Mohammed is a symbol of human perfection and the ideal for human society. Nasr in his book on Islam states, "The Prophet in these qualities that he displayed so eminently is at once the prototype of human and spiritual perfection and a guide towards its realization.[6] He describes the Prophet as having had an active social life. He was married, maintained a household, was a father, a ruler and a judge and a warrior. He experienced many hardships as well as the joys and despair implicit in the human condition. He was contemplative. He was kind and gentle but harsh in the face of injustice. He was noble and generous, loving, compassionate and pious.

The Prophet was combative. Internally he was continuously fighting against all man's nature which kept him from God's will, and externally he was prepared to combat anything which negated his truth and disrupted harmony.

He had a great love and magnanimity toward his companions. He was generous and demonstrated this by continually doing for and giving of himself to others. He gave freely, asked for nothing. Nasr comments,

> In Islam, when one thinks of the Prophet who is to be emulated, it is the image of a strong personality that comes to mind, who is severe with himself and with the false and unjust, and charitable towards the world that surrounds him. On the basis of these two virtues of strength and sobriety on the one hand and charity and generosity on the other, he is serene, extinguished in the Truth. He is that warrior on horseback who halts before the mountain of Truth, passive toward the Divine Will, active toward the world, hard and sober towards himself and kind and generous towards the creatures about him[6]

The Way of Judaism

More flesh, more worms;
More wealth, more worry;
More women, more witchcraft;
More concubines, more lechery;
More slaves, more thievery.
(But) More Law, more life;
More study, more wisdom;
More counsel, more enlightenment,
More righteousness, more peace.

— The Talmud (from Mishna)

Four classes of men will never see God's face: the scoffer, the liar,
the slanderer, and the hypocrite.

a1— *The Talmud (Satah, 24a)*

Choose life, that you may live, you and your descendants.

— Deuteronomy 30:19

Judaism, though comprising the belief system of but a half of one percent of the world's population, is one of the world's most important religious philosophies and basic to both Islam and Christianity. As such, it affects the life of almost fifty percent of personkind.

Judaism had its tribal and ritualistic origins among a nomadic, pastoral, Semetic people called Hebrews. In the hands of several fiery prophets, it grew as a prophetic religion with a strong human ethic. The teachings were formed into a single canon with three divisions: the Torah (the law), the Neviim (Prophets), and the Kitubien (the Writings) — the Christians later called this canon "The Old Testament."

Also sacred among the Jews was a secondary group of writings known as the Apocrypha and the Talmud.

All of these works are moral and ethical in nature and directly related to the human person. Thus, Judaism is important for the purpose of this discussion. It dramatically represents a people's persistant struggle to achieve a more noble life and create a happier world for all.

In essence, in Judaism, the person is created in the image of God. Thus, man is not sinful in nature, but good. The world, of course, offers constant temptations but Jews do not renunciate an active participation in that world. Rather, because of the temptations, their major task is to raise themselves and the workaday world in which they move to the highest level possible so that each of their acts reflect the divine unity of all things.

In Mishnah, Avat 3:15, it is written "Everything is foreseen by God, and freedom of choice is given to man." With freedom of choice, then, all followers of Judaism are responsible for their lives, their actions and for the society which they create. All of these will require personal choice. Their guides are the holy books. They can only blame themselves for wrong choices, misdeeds, transgressions and loss of self.

Jews cannot be apathetic about existence. They are *commanded* to choose life. They are made fully aware that life is pain, despair and evil. "There is not a single one among you who is not guilty of many sins." (Tanhuma [Burber] Hukkut 39). But suffering is not meaningless. Accepting suffering as the person's lot in life without question, as in the book of Job, can bring peace, unity and understanding. But, on the other hand, Jews are encouraged to live their lives fully, actively, joyfully and enthusiastically." At judgment day every man will have to give account for every good thing which he might have enjoyed and did not." (Jerusalem Kiddrishin, 66d)

The code for human behavior in Judaism is clearly stated in all of the holy books, especially the Torah. It is here where the most honored code of behavior in all the world is found, "The Ten Commandments." It seems hardly necessary that they be stated here for they form a behavioral code which is universally known.

The way of Jewish life is not only spelled out in the commandments but in every major division of the holy canon. Jews are told how to behave in such diverse life situations as burials, visitations of the sick, counseling the young and respecting the aged. They are encouraged to live in gentleness, wisdom, continual learning, family unity, humility, reverence, modesty and continual self-examination. They are told the value of self-reliance and warned against becoming addicted to "the broken reed of human support," or human praise.

They are warned against the false security which comes from hoarding gold and encouraged to be charitable to all. It is recommended that Jews live their lives as if they were always standing in the presence of their God; for it is only in this world, not in any world to come, that they will have the possibility to choose their own way and justify their God-given life.

For the Jew, it is life that must be actualized, and this can only be achieved through actively participating in life. "Whatever a man does not do while he has the power granted him by his Creator, the power of freedom of will, which is his all the days of his life, during which he is free and responsible, he will not be able to do in the grave or in Shoel, where he will not have this power." (Moses Luzatto, Yesharian, Chapter 4)

Jews are lovers; lovers of God, of nature, of people and of life. To them, the Torah spells out how to live their loving way in wisdom. Its words are *life giving* and *love giving*. It teaches them to love themselves, and all things. It teaches them charity and sets down the laws of giving and sharing and love of the land.

In essence, Judaism sees its followers as having great dignity and innate power, as well as limitless possibilities. They are responsible creatures of piety with a deep reverence for life and a great spirituality. They are asked to live as a continual emanation of God. They have a deep respect for learning and the learned. They believe in the grandeur and goodness of their own inner nature. They are comfortable with mysticism and see life as both a mystery not to be explained and a reality over which they have volitional control and may discover in action.

Elie Wiesel, in his stunning and moving novel, *Souls On Fire,* seems to best sum up the goal of the fully active person living in Judaism. He quotes the words of the great rabbi, Menahem-Mendl of Vitebak who said, "My mission on earth is to recognize the void — inside and outside of me — and fill it!"

The Way of Christianity

Therefore thou art inexcusable, O man, whosoever thou
art that judgest; for wherein thou judgest, thou
condemnest thyself; for you that judgest doeth the same
things.

—The Epistle of Paul
Romans 2:1-2

But I say unto you which hear, love your enemies, do
good to them which hate you,
Bless them that curse you, and pray for them which
despitefully use you.
And unto him that smiteth thee on the one cheek offer
also the other; and him that taketh away thy cloak
forbid not to take thy coat also.
Give every man that asketh of thee, and of him that
taketh away thy goods ask them not again.
And as ye would that men should do to you, do ye
also to them likewise.

—Luke 6:27-31

Know ye not that ye are the temple of God,
and that the spirit of God dwelleth in you?
If any man defile the temple of God, him
shall God destroy: for the temple of God
is holy, which temple ye are.

I Corinthians 3:16,17

Christianity forms the faith of nearly 600 million people today, approximately thirty percent of the entire human race. More than half of these are Catholics, a fourth of them Protestants of various sects and the remainder form a myriad of other orthodoxies. No religion in the world is more widespread.

Christianity had its humble beginnings among a small group of individuals, mostly peasants, led by a remarkable Jewish prophet named Jesus of Nazareth. Many believed Him to be the long awaited Messiah. In His brief life on earth He gave His followers renewed joy, hope, faith and love through a living example of His perfectionist doctrines.

After His death, His beliefs were gathered together into several scriptures which have been highly influential in guiding the ethics of the daily lives of millions of people the world over. His canon was referred to as the New Testament and together with the Old Testament became known as The Bible (The Book).

Since the days of Jesus of Nazareth, the history of Christianity has been one of varying and thoughtful controversy. Though firmly based upon essential dogma which remains basically unchanged, and gathering its energies from Christian revelation, the source of which is the Bible, differing formal institutions have emerged to meet the ever-changing history of the human condition. Several different churches have evolved, some of which divided into denominations, sects and National Churches. Still, with Jesus Christ, the Man, as the perfect example, there has been little controversy regarding what is the Christian life. It is with this, rather than the differing pedogogy and structures of the institutionalized churches, which is of interest here.

Christianity states that God is in all of us at each moment of our lives and, in addition, there is always more to be realized in our future. The gospel of John 17:21 states, "even as thou, Father, art in me, and I in thee, that they also may be in us." By implication this suggests an ideal self, a human perfection to which the person can aspire, an unending process which, if followed, eventually transcends the self, time and space. Practically, it is based upon perfect faith, love, joy, peace, forgiveness, gentleness and continual growth. This stimulates its followers to becoming internally and externally integrated. It suggests a harmony within the person, nature and God and an ongoing and continual harmonizing of all three.

Jesus represents also the focus of human maturity. He reveals to His followers the true human nature. He becomes the focus of their philosophy of life. As such, He is looked upon by Christians as the greatest teacher of "The Way," and offers them the rules and regulations for becoming a fully functioning human person.

Christians accept their life, no matter what its outward manifestation, on faith. They are offered choices. Their life decisions are to be made according to their understanding of God's will. As such, they select from alternatives which their unique lives offer them and deal squarely with each new challenge. They will be, in this way, fully responsible for their choices. Faith, since it is integrated as one's inner life, granted by God, becomes the major source of energy in decision making and therefore requires that one be in constant touch with one's inner forces.

Human nature and real life become the raw material for Christian character. Since growing persons are responsible for their lives, are imperfect and not without fault, they often make wrong choices. At these times they become alienated from their true selves and the world and may no longer trust their own judgment. Or, too, they may know the right way and select not to take it. In this case the Church becomes a source for leading them from darkness, ignorance and selfishness to more appropriate ways of acting and responding.

True Christians know who they are. They have a strong sense of identity which defies political power, material wealth and worldly pleasure. As the apostle Paul described himself in II Corinthians 4:8-9, "afflicted in every way, but not crushed; perplexed, but not driven to despair; persecuted, but not forsaken; struck down, but not destroyed." This strong identity offers Christians, as Tillich suggests, "The Courage to Be." It offers them the basic right to be the unique responsible person that they are and function as best they can in congruence with the world and the self.

While the inward essence of Christianity lies in faith, its external expression is love. At the heart of Christian love is self-giving. The fulfillment of selfhood lies in transcending the self. This is epitomized in Christianity by the symbol of the cross upon which Christ was murdered. It represents the pattern for Christian humanism for it breaks through with liberating strength demanding nothing but always forgetting and forgiving. There are no strings attached to Christian love. It is freely offered in the hope that it will be freely received.

Also basic to Christian love is the integrity of all persons. It respects their basic dignity and their right to their own personalities. It implies an ever increasing need to know oneself, and participate in an ever expanding awareness through growth in sensitivity, freedom and relatedness.

The spirit of Christian love has no place for self-contempt, self-pity or self-humiliation, for Christians strongly believe in their ability to transcend themselves.

Christian love is also manifest in a relatedness with others Self-love and love for others are identical. In the expression "love thy neighbor as thyself" one senses the unification of self and others.

Christians are integrated and humble. Like Christ they identify with the hungry, the thirsty, the naked, the sick and the oppressed. Christ did this without losing His divinity. His example was in His approach to people. It was always practical and concrete. He fed the hungry, comforted the sad and healed the sick. He became "the partner" of the human person and wished the person to become "His partner." In this way He gave the person an understanding of love as openness, universality, mutual and self-respect, harmony and transcendence of self.

From the Christian point of view, then, true Christians represent integrated individuals who are at home on earth and with forces greater than themselves. They are eager to participate in the course of history in unity, harmony and love. They are knowing, feeling, willing individuals. They are conscious of the self and its significance. They are capable of realizing ideals, and appreciate values such as love, truth, beauty and goodness. They are compelled to become what they can and ought to be, for they know that in a very special sense, they bear the image of their Creator.

As can be observed after reading this chapter, there is little dissonance among the several philosophical and religious systems in their suggestions as to what it means to live in full humanness. If we look at human behavior in our world today it becomes especially obvious that there is often a great deal of dissonance between ascribing to an ethical system and genuinely living it in day-to-day practice. But, this need not be so. With some degree of creativity, intelligence, diligence and choice, the way of the fully functioning person is clear, consistant in the main and has been accomplished by personkind in the past. The overall, overriding code seems to arise from what has been scoffed at as a supreme and simplistic platitude, "Do unto others as you would have them do unto you." To this I would add, "Give unto God and the world all that you are and all that you can be."

Perhaps, as Gore Vidal says, "All truth is platitude and all platitude is truth." The tragedy is that it takes us a lifetime to learn this.

GROWING AS THE
FULLY FUNCTIONING PERSON

We do not exist for ourselves (as the center of the universe), and it is only when we are fully convinced of this fact that we begin to love ourselves properly and thus also love others. What do I mean by loving ourselves properly? I mean, first of all, desiring to live, accepting life as a very great gift and a great good, not because of what it gives us, but because of what it enables us to give others.

Thomas Merton

CHAPTER 4

Except for some rather vague, broad and nebulous guidelines, none of us is ever taught how to live. We are not told the value of life nor what it means to be fully alive. We have no idea of the wonders we can take from life or of the responsibility we have to give it something in return. We are born into our world, educated to adjust to it according to the dominant and accepted mores and then pretty much left to sink or swim.

There is no school for living, and a dearth of teachers of life. If we look to formal education for answers, we are most often given knowledge without judgment and facts without meaning. If we expect answers from religion we are often persuaded to make the leap into faith, for which many of us are sorely unprepared. When we are incapable of complying, we are often made to feel incompetent and dependent. If we try to learn from life itself we find that often it seems full of unforeseen dirty tricks for which we are not ready and from which we seem to glean little. If we attempt to learn from examples, we find too few models.

It is only when we can no longer cope and fall under the pain and strain of nonfulfillment that we are forced to obtain some help or make some change. Usually this is simply a token adjustment — vague and temporary — before we are returned to "real" life, as ill prepared as before.

We are faced with the reality that if we wish to live fully and in harmony with life, we will have to become self-motivated students. We will have to be ready to risk, look inside ourselves, and proceed through trial and error. The job will be mainly ours. We will be required to be our own mentors.

Since we are all different there can be no one way. But it does help to assume a few prerequisites. For instance, we must seriously decide to start on our way and to stay on our path. We must view ourselves as products of our past but more importantly, as having a rich and unlimited future which does not necessarily depend upon what has come before. We must form an intimate alliance with hope, not the illusionary variety of hope, but the kind which gives strength and practical direction. We must regain our respect for our uniqueness of mind and power of will so that we may utilize them to aid us in examining and selecting the most sound and growth-producing alternatives among the many choices the future will offer. Then, we must dedicate ourselves to the process with sensitive and honest evaluation at each step. Armed with strength and choice we are ready to look at some ways in which we might better become the orchestrators of our lives and live each day as fully active and functioning persons.

The Role of Death

He who isn't busy being born is busy dying.

—Bob Dylan

Perhaps the fact of life most conducive to living fully as a person is an honest awareness and acceptance of death.

Death has no secrets. If we are willing to look, it constantly makes us aware of itself. It is everywhere, even at the first sign of life.

Children seem to have some personal fantasy of death as early as they can conceptualize, though it is not until they are approximately nine years old that they seem to be able to verbalize its true nature and especially accept its finality. Still, death is shrouded in its own mystery. One can never know beforehand precisely how or when it will come. No matter how prepared we are, it always seems to take us by surprise. Even forewarned we seem unable to contend with the shock or accept it without experiencing deep feelings of fear, superstition, anxiety and isolation. It's always the other person who dies. The dead are not even permitted to remain dead — they are too often resurrected through the guilt of the living.

When one is fully functioning as a person, death is neither a threat nor a horror. Rather, it serves as life's greatest ally. Death tells us that we must live life now, in the moment — that tomorrow is illusion and never comes. It tells us that it is not the quantity of our days, or hours, or years that matter, but rather the quality of the time spent. Every day is new. Every moment is fresh. Time has no meaning in itself unless we choose to give it significance. Moments pass swiftly or as

Perhaps the fact of life most conducive to living fully as a person is an honest awareness and acceptance of death.

eternities depending upon our state of mind — or rather how we are willing to suspend our minds. It is often said that there are those who can experience more in a moment than some can experience in a lifetime. Time is relative. It is ours, given freely to spend wisely or to squander idly, but never to be hoarded. Time past is gone and all the moaning will never bring it back. Perhaps the most irresponsible phrase in the language is "I should have." The main import of the past is simply as a source of learning through experience. But even then our learning can at best be general. Since each experience has new and different significance, it can only be used in a vague and general sense when applied to the future. But the future, too, is illusion, a type of dream which in most cases never comes to pass as dreamed. So much of our pain is based upon the disappointment of the reality not living up to the dream.

Death also teaches us the impermanence of all things. All things change. All things die. This is true in nature as well as in human life. Even granite mountains crumble into dust just as the most beautiful of past kingdoms have left only silent stones to surround their mystery. To be attached to things or people, both of which will surely vanish, can only bring despair, for eventually one is left with only a handful of dust or a frail memory. Life that is free of attachment lives in the moment and makes no demand that the moment last. Life's concern is not with the future but with the present. To wait for life is to love to wait, nothing more. Life understands that death brings with it change and that the only reality is to live both the future and the past in the present, accepting it with

95

the joy of the moment and letting it go when the time is right; embracing it with all one's energies before it leaves, but without expectations of permanency. As has been noted earlier, the Buddhists teach the futility of attachments of any kind and see them as being at the root of all suffering. They say that as long as we remain attached we will live despairingly. They speak of three types of attachment states — attached, unattached and nonattached. They tell a beautiful tale which illustrates their meaning. They ask us to visualize ourselves in a very isolated situation where the only fresh water available must be carried from a great distance (a common situation in many Asian towns and monasteries). Water is therefore treated as a most precious commodity. It is placed in a large pot, used sparingly, and kept shaded under trees, guarded and carefully covered.

After having worked hard all day in the blazing sun — we look forward to that refreshing stop at the water pot. We lift the lid carefully, take the scooper in hand and dip into the precious liquid. As we are about to drink we notice an ant has somehow settled into our pot and onto our scooper. We are furious! How dare the ant be on our island, under our trees, in our water pot, on our scooper. We immediately crush it under our thumb.
Attached.

Or we might stop a moment to consider that it is a hot day even for ants. The ant has done what is instinctively right for it—it took refuge in the only cool, damp and comfortable place it could find. We see that the ant is not really harming our water, our trees, our scooper or our

pot. After deep, moral consideration, we drink around it, replace the scooper in the cool pot and cover it carefully.
Unattached.

Or, when we see the ant in our pot we stop neither to consider what is the ant's or what is ours, nor what is moral or immoral. We respond above morality. We naturally feed it a lump of sugar!
Nonattached.

Death teaches us that in the long run nothing belongs to us. Even if we desire to form permanent attachments or possess, we in truth cannot. Things will break in spite of us. People will depart when it is their time no matter how loudly we protest. Ants will invade our water pots with no regard to our barriers. A knowledge of death can give one a deep feeling of freedom — both from attachment to self, as well as attachment to others and to things. The less we are attached to, the less we have to worry about.

The last words my mother ever spoke to me were very insightful. As I stood quietly weeping at her bedside, she lovingly took my hand and said, "Felice, what are *you* holding on to?" I let go and it made all the difference to both of us. We even attach a sense of guilt to the dying for leaving us!

Death is too often bound and gagged. Children are discouraged from attending funerals and given meager answers to their questions regarding it. Death is kept a dark, frightening and often totally devastating mystery, as if it were some intruder to be excluded at any cost.

I recall my extreme shock and horror upon arriving in Benares, India, for the first time. There before me was

When we can embrace death as simply another aspect of the life cycle, we will give appreciation and value to each life encounter knowing that it will never occur again.

unmasked pain, hunger, and blatant death. A parade of exposed cadavers were moving continually down the crowded streets toward the Holy River Ganges. Everyone watched as bodies were publicly cremated in colorful ceremony. The streets were lined with the crippled, lepers and beggers. When I recovered from my first impression of horror, I began to find mothers with shining eyes nursing their smiling infants, glowing smiles on the faces of old men and women, unbridled joy in young boys and girls who sprinted along the streets and a spiritual sense of peace and acceptance on faces such as I had never before witnessed. What I was seeing was the panorama of life — all at once, nothing hidden. I realized how sheltered I had been all my previous years. It is the Western way for most people to experience their real existence almost entirely behind closed windows and locked doors. We cry alone, we become ill alone, we are born alone and most of us will die in some sterile hospital room, alone. How can we know or accept the natural cycle of life when it has been so hidden from us? How can we ever learn? How can we ever accept?

When we can embrace death as simply another aspect of the life cycle, we will give appreciation and value to each life encounter knowing that it will never occur again. And each of these moments will be the source of what we shall know as our lifetime.

Death is the greatest of life's teachers. It is only the ignorant and those who are afraid to live who fear it. The wise accept Death as their intimate friend and most gracious teacher. To be fully active and fully functioning as a person we must make death a lifelong friend.

The Role of Self Determination

Love not what you are but only what you may become.

— Cervantes

Each of us is a separate person. We are the subtle combination of factors which are never likely to occur again. We are all singular and incomparable. Who and what we are has been determined largely by our heredity, society, education, family and friends. All of these have helped to make our lives richer and more exciting. But they have also brought with them complications, frustrations, and contradictions which have made severe demands upon our mental and emotional energies and which are likely to continue to do so in the future. It was in this way that our personhood was created, both by the rich and exciting as well as the frustrating and depressing. Somewhere, within and between both, will lie our true selves.

As fully functioning persons we know that we have a right to be what we are, even if what we are is not compatible with what we have learned to be. We have a right to choose our own selves, even if that self is different from the selves of others. We have a right to feel as we do even if those feelings are frowned upon by others. This does not mean that we have a right to inflict ourselves upon others any more than we would desire to have others inflict themselves upon us. It does mean that we have a right to choose, develop and live congruently with ourselves and to share without apology.

A poem which states this powerfully and simply has the impressive title,

"I am neither a sacrilege nor a privilege
i may not be competent or excellent
but I am present"

Michele, the young poetess, states boldly,

My happiness is me
not you
Not only because you may be temporary
But also because you want me to be
What I am not.
I cannot be happy when I change
Merely to satisfy your selfishness
Nor can I feel content
When you criticize me for not thinking
Your thoughts for not seeing
like you. You call me a rebel
Yet for each time I have rejected
Your beliefs, you have rebelled against mine.
I do not try to mold your mind
I know you are trying hard enough to be just you
And I cannot allow you to tell me what to be
For I am concentrating on being me.

She adds,

You said i was transparent
And easily forgotten
But why then did you try to use my lifetime
To prove to yourself what you are?

Indeed we are our own happiness and each time we have strayed from ourselves we have been led to despair. We cannot find ourselves in others. We cannot live for others nor can we use them for our own self-affirmation. We cannot always be what others want us to be, for what they want may not be what we are and that is all that we have. We can only rely upon ourselves. This is such a simple fact, yet it is perhaps the greatest single cause of human psychological struggle and pain. It is often easier for us to become what others desire but in so doing we relinquish our dreams, abandon our hopes and ignore our needs. This leaves us feeling abandoned, weakened and impotent, without a genuine self. We have all we need to become what we are, our perfect selves. All we need to do to realize it is to recognize it, develop it and live it in action. We must embrace ourselves as we are and as we have the potential to become before we can embrace life or others. We must yield to the pull toward self-realization in a way which is good, loving, peaceful, joyful, patient and disciplined. We must have no desire to control, possess or dominate nor allow others to do so to us. Armed with the daring to turn inward and freed from the tyranny of externality, we must determine our way. We must affirm ourselves. We continue to gain the wisdom and strength and freedom to accept as well as reject, to instigate change or remain static, to affect others as well as be affected by them, to determine circumstances as well as be at their mercy. We are no longer puppets being manipulated by outside powerful forces; we become the powerful force ourselves.

For all human acts there are alternatives. The greater the

number of imaginative and creative alternatives to behavior we possess, the more meaningful the choice, the more self determined the action. Some persons, for example, find that the only escape from despair lies in such drastic and limited behaviors as murder, suicide or madness; others become almost totally impotent to act. There are those who seem to be able to survive anything — experience the pain, feel the hurt, know the fear, then let it go and continue to function. The more mentally ill the person, the fewer the alternatives. The more fully functioning the person, the more vast the choices. Life is selected over death, wisdom over ignorance, pain over apathy and joy over despair. They use themselves and their environment to the best advantage.

No one who is trying to be themselves will ever be free from tragedy. External circumstances will forever continue to frustrate us on our way. We are so conditioned to the expectation of the worst that we have become suspicious of peace, joy and love and are certain that when we experience joy, horror must be just around the corner. We cannot stop a hurricane, silence a storm or keep a loved one from leaving us. But it is our response and reaction to these catastrophic experiences that will determine whether we will continue to survive and grow toward becoming a fully functioning person. This is another way of saying that fully functioning persons use pain and joy equally in determining themselves. They can either relinquish the responsibility for their lives to outside forces such as society, family, friends or lovers, or they can assume the bittersweet responsibility of their own self-creation.

The Role of Connectiveness

No man is an island of itself. Each is a piece of the continent a part of the main

— John Donne

Just as fully functioning persons write the script of their own lives, they also respect the connectiveness of all things along the way. They realize that the self is only the self in that it has a world, a structure of which it is a part — a part, yet apart. We are a community of persons and a world of things. We are what we are because birds exist, plants grow, bees pollinate, winds blow, tides change, rains fall, and accidents happen. Nothing occurs in the world that in some way does not affect us all. Even the most insignificant act we perform will have some effect upon the world.

Philosophers talk of all of us being caught up and moving in a single stream of life. We all originated from the source but are not ourselves the source. We arise as a special quality of the source and pass on into it again while the true source itself remains. We will run our unique way, over rapids, peaceful ponds, fiercely at times, calmly at others. We will join other streams and rivers along the way, gaining strength, being propelled or momentarily falling aside in muddy, stagnant pools. But no matter how quickly or slowly or quietly or passionately we move, we all come eventually to the same end in the same sea. We have returned to the source from which we rose. We are therefore at one time or another, the beginning, the end, as well as the way, but are *permanently* never any of them. We are an important part of the dynamic process, but we, like everything else, are only passing through. We are each a singular person but we are each a universal person as well. Both are equally important. We are born provincial, egocentric, limited. The more we become, the more universal the person we are. We finally come to realize that most human conflicts arise through our provincialism, our concern for our personal problems, our selfish interests, our own conflicts.

Most of us define a good day as one in which all things have gone *our* way. We see the good life as one in which *our* personal dreams have been realized. It is not our concern if thousands go to bed each night hungry and in despair, as long as they keep out of sight and leave us alone. It doesn't matter to us if the world's children are being battered or not being educated properly. Our children are fully grown and doing well, and we have no responsibility for the others. It is only when we are mugged by the hungry children or brutalized or terrorized in our home that we realize the connectiveness of all things. There is no place to hide. No one is guilty. We are all innocents in an ever changing stream for which each of us is responsible. It is a fantasy to believe that peace comes without all of us moving together with the stream in unity, joy, wonder and love. An English poet, Francis Thompson once wrote that he could not pick a flower without troubling a star.

A bush grows. The blowing wind, gliding birds and busy insects gather the pollen to sow it again miles from the original flowering plant. We pass, unsuspecting, on a morning's stroll. We, too, gather the pollen on our clothes and unsuspectingly carry the plant to spread its life beauty to new uncharted areas. The flower is born from the same source, journeys along the same path, momentarily uses our nurturing and understanding to continue on its way. Without us it would pass into oblivion, and we would deny all who follow the comfort and wisdom of the flowers.

In some way, however small and secret, we are all dependent one upon the other. Fully functioning persons recognize this power and know that it stems from the source which is able to create light or produce darkness. A word, an act, an expressed feeling can reverberate in wide circles in the pond — touching unsuspecting travellers. Our mood at the start of a day can affect all those with whom we will come into contact. The river runs its course. We cannot escape moving together and affecting whatever we encounter. The collective actualization of the trip is put into jeopardy by even one person's nonbeing.

The Role of Purpose

*He who enters the sphere of faith (the state of being ultimately concerned)
enters into the sanctuary of life.*

— Paul Tillich

Perhaps the purpose of life is to forward it by being
something, having it make a difference that our unique selves
were present. The existentialist says "to be is to do." Fully
functioning persons realize that it is in the productive act
itself in which the power and significance of being
"individual" is present.

We are all involved in a type of progressive evolution. It is
only through us, through our uniqueness and production
that we, humanity, can become involved in the ethics of
growth. The basis of this is a belief in action. In some way,
each of us has something to offer, some contribution to make
to the productive process. Too many of us see ourselves as
useless and worthless — and certainly without the ability to
offer anything to our world. We select to be followers rather
than leaders. We become conformists rather than have the
courage to be ourselves and create newness through the
expression of those selves. We, in this way, lose ourselves,
and in so doing, the world, too, experiences the loss of us.

One of the requirements to be met in my university classes
is that all the students do something in the community, for
somebody else, free of salary and mostly under self-
supervision. This often produces great anxiety. Questions
arise such as "What is there to do?", "What can I do?" The
tragedy in the lives of most of us is that we are so isolated and

Whatever immortality there is, is assured by a continual participation in the productive process.

so far from awareness of pain that when we are given statistics concerning despair, hunger, crime and useless loss of potential, it is easy for us to remain detached and even deny the facts from our conscious minds. This became painfully apparent as we listened to the unemotional narration of death statistics during the Vietnam conflict. The rather apathetic professional announcer would recite "Nine hundred and seventy Vietnamese were killed in battle this past week. Only 330 U.S. troops were killed during the same period!" Good Grief! Thirteen hundred human lives!

A few years ago a young man, Joel, confused over my assignment, came to my office. He could not imagine what there was for him to do in the local community. What need could it have of him?

After some discussion I escorted him to a local convalescent home with which I had recently communicated regarding volunteer help. A brief tour answered the question of need. Old people, looking half crazed with boredom and uselessness stared about the dull rooms in apathy. Some wandered in loose, soiled white pajamas or gowns, from one place to another, as if looking for a space that was not empty.

"What's there to do?" I asked.

Joel started with a one-day-a-week visit to the bedside of an old woman whose family had all but abandoned her to age and death. His presence attracted others, equally lonely, to chat with this strong, healthy young man. His day began to be referred to as "Joel's day."

Joel's apprehension over having no skills soon vanished. It

became apparent that it was enough to be present and be himself. The old woman began to dress for his visit. She had her once stringy hair done and tinted an ever-so-pale blue. The men on the ward, too, began to put on shirt and trousers and enter into the animated activities and conversations.

Joel's day was voluntarily extended to three days a week. The change in the home, from such a seemingly small thing, was beautifully obvious. The joyful culmination was watching Joel, like the Pied Piper, leading a procession of halting but happy senior citizens through the campus, heading for a basketball game, a play or concert.

All experiences of doing are not as dramatic as this. But from it, Joel learned that there *was* a need and that *he* could meet a part of it. He selected a career (in which he is presently most successful) in the helping professions.

Each act makes *us* manifest. It is what we do, rather than what we feel, or say we do, that reflects who and what we truly are. Each of our acts makes a statement as to our purpose. Whatever immortality there is, is assured by a continual participation in the productive process. Because of us, things have become more. Something has been left of significance because we existed.

This does not mean that we can only find significance by winning Nobel Prizes or engaging in world-shaking inventions, life-saving exploits or artistic triumphs. It does mean doing the thing which is uniquely ours to do, whatever that may be, and doing it well. We need not be a Salk, Curie,

Jefferson, a Keller, or King in order to give to the world. Ms. Smith or Mr. Jones, neither of whom will ever receive national recognition, or for that matter ever read their names in print, can also leave their indelible and significant marks upon the world. Anything which leads to good, to joy, to understanding, to acceptance is significant. It is this knowledge of one's ability to contribute to a universal, continual and infinite productivity, that adds special meaning to our lives and the courage of our mortality.

The Role of Communication

Fully functioning persons are eager to communicate.

Perhaps the most difficult, yet vitally essential aspect of living as a fully functioning human among other human beings is the ability to communicate. No one can know us unless we are willing and able to tell them through our actions, as well as our words, who we are. We must be constantly engaged in verbalizing through language, gesture, or action our ever changing selves. The alternatives to this lie in confusion, anxiety and aloneness. Loneliness and misunderstandings arise from our inability to present ourselves honestly and authentically in each new encounter. An interesting illustration of this occurred in a Love class I was facilitating. During a particular session, a dog entered the room. He unhesitatingly approached the group, wagging his tail in the joy of having discovered so much potential for love. His need was, as he had expected, satisfied by each student he approached. As he received the caresses he desired, still wagging his tail and flashing his trusting eyes, he moved on to the next person. The class proceeded without interruption when suddenly a young lady shouted from the rear of the group "Damn!" This outburst succeeded in giving her the undivided attention she required. She added, "I can't believe it! I've been sitting here in desperate loneliness wanting someone to see or touch me, but it hasn't happened. Every one of you has been indifferent to my needs. I could die here of loneliness. A dog comes in, and immediately the whole group shares its love and caresses! That's incredible!" "Well," responded a young man not too far away, "perhaps we did that because the dog let us know that he was lovable. He wagged his tail and came to us with inviting eyes. I saw you sitting there when I first came into the room. My perception of you was as someone cool, collected and self-centered. You didn't seem to require anything, least of all for me to touch you. Maybe the secret lies in letting people know honestly what you need before you accuse them of being indifferent. After all, we're not mind readers."

"Well, then, hear me!" she added, "I do need!" And as she stated this she got on all fours, dog fashion, and with trusting eyes and a valiant attempt at wagging her tail, she passed through the group. Needless to say, she was petted by everyone.

But communication is not always so simple. Words can also be traps. We must be certain that when we are communicating we know precisely what we want to express. Vagueness leads only to fear and insecurity. If we were asked by someone to specifically define the terms we use, could we do it? Not without some difficulty. Few can. How can we then blame others for misunderstanding what we are only vaguely able to express ourselves?

Fully functioning persons are aware of the pitfalls of communication and therefore do not take it casually. They listen to the words they speak and those spoken to them.

They attempt to find the most exact and least threatening words for communicating themselves. They strive to put these words into the most succinct context so that they can be assured of as little misunderstanding as possible. They often paraphrase what they think they have heard or encourage the listener to *rephrase* what they have said, so that they can have feedback as reinforcement of intention. That is why there is much wisdom in the statement that "the wise person never has short arguments"!

We all have the right to make our statement, have it heard and understood. But unless we are content to talk to ourselves, we will only know who we are and others will only know who we are, when we are able to say what we mean.

The Role of Doubt and Uncertainty

The most beautiful thing we can experience is the mystery.
                                                          Albert Einstein

Existence is frail and changeable. It is always unpredictable and full of doubt. But this doubt need not be negative. If all things were known about our lives much of the magic would be gone. Doubt brings with it the element of surprise, of continual newness. Sensitive and intelligent people are always full of doubt. They see it as a positive influence for spontaneity and continued growth. It is the element of uncertainty that adds the spice to living. How different life would be if we could predict tomorrow with moment-to-moment accuracy. How dull would be our world. How soon we would lose interest, cease dreaming, become bored. But life is not like that. It is always full of questions. It shows us dramatically that we can be certain of nothing. We cannot be sure of what the next moment will bring. This causes most of us to spend a large portion of our lives engaged in worrying about possible outcomes, most of which are beyond our control. It doesn't seem to matter that much of what we worry about never seems to happen anyway...we continue to choose to worry.

All of us have felt, at some time or another, that if things and people were more predictable we would finally find some peace and security. In actuality, we would discover no such dream state, for there is no permanence, no assurance, no forever. All is impermanent and in constant change. In fact, that is what is meant by the process of life.

Even knowing this, most of us still strive to overcome

doubt by becoming professional planners. We relentlessly schedule for months and even years in advance. We desire to be assured of the future. Certainly there is some joy to be found in planning and even some necessity for it, but more often then not, as Burns says, "The best laid schemes o' mice and men gang oft a-gley; an lea'e us not but grief and pain, for promis'd joy." Things seldom occur the way they are planned. Unrealized dreams are the main cause of useless pain. Perhaps if we would be more willing to allow people, situations and tomorrow to tell their own tales, they might bring a new element of serendipity into our highly-structured lives. Too, they might help us to avoid much useless worry and disappointment.

Doubt and uncertainty cause us to often engage in the process of seeking externally for strength and controls. We amass fortunes, frantically climb power ladders, collect prestigious titles, all in the hope of overcoming our fear of the unknown and acquiring some feeling of security. We secretly admire the powerful, emulate the successful and seek out those who appear secure. We are convinced that if we had their money, their fame or their strength, our fears and doubts would vanish. But we are devastated to learn that when we do have more wealth, when fame is ours, when we become all powerful, nothing much has changed. We simply have acquired new anxieties and different doubts. Life, and the world, by its very nature will always remain a puzzle. There is no alternative but to accept it as it is. Therein lies the only certitude, that we can only be certain about uncertainty.

To be fully functioning, then, we must be as welcoming of the new as we are comfortable with the old, as fearless of the unexpected as we are falsely secure in the planned.

The Role of Spirituality

Nothing here below is profane for those who know how to see. On the contrary everything is sacred.

Teilhard de Chardin

Fully functioning persons have a deep sense of spirituality. They know that their personhood and the world in which they live cannot be explained or understood through human experience alone. They know that they must make the "mystical leap." They must go beyond themselves, beyond their limited reality. They have an inexplicable sense of something more. They feel a greater operative intellect than their own, even if they are at a loss to give it a name. They are aware of a great design, incessantly operative, in which all is compatible and in which there are no contradictions.

Life offers us few explanations. We cannot be certain of the true meaning of life, the source of life nor life after life. Only we can fill the void which this incertitude creates. We can either accept in faith or select nothingness. Both engage us in mystery. Either we select to believe that everything matters or nothing matters — yet, in essence, both are the same. Both will involve mind games, for neither offer definitive proofs. This does not mean that answers do not exist. It is like the Zen Koan which states that there is no difference if we think we are the monk dreaming we are a butterfly or a butterfly dreaming we are a monk dreaming we are a butterfly.

Some of us are unable to live without answers. The void is too totally frightening, too devastating. So we must create answers for ourselves. Some of us choose to live without answers. We find them unnecessary. We live out our lives without asking questions, living into answers. Both ways require the creating of a belief system for which there is no validation. Either choice embodies a living sense of spirituality which arises from the affirmation of the self through personal choice itself.

Spirituality, faith and mystery are inherent in every aspect of life. I recall when I visited New England and had my first experience with the grandeur of fall. I had never seen trees in such a prismatic blaze of color. What impressed me most was that on the same tree there would be leaves which varied from bright yellow to deep purple, often on the same branch. I recall turning to my friends in puzzlement and awe, and asking why. They had lived in the area all of their lives and could not answer me. "That's just the way it is," they offered. That was a fine answer but not enough for me. Surely someone more knowledgeable than I had asked the same question and arrived at a more enlightening and "scientific" explanation. Yes, there was such an answer. There were botanical explanations which involved position of the individual leaf to the sun and shade, as well as frost factor. All of these were explained stunningly but I left the library none the less overwhelmed, none the less awed. The scientific answer had not taken the mystery from the experience. Because something can be explained need not affect its wonder!

We can predict tides almost to the second. We can date and time the migration of birds and whales. We can walk on the moon. But does this lessen the wonder of the sea, the magic of birds or the beauty of the planets?

To be in touch with nature, to feel deeply its moods, to experience fully its sorcery, to know how so-called "inanimate" things work, is to become caught up in the spirituality and divinity of all things. I have never been able to take the *common* for granted and am still thrilled when I dial a telephone direct, across the United States or to Europe, and hear the person I am calling answer, almost immediately, "hello" or "pronto" or "mushi mushi." The fact that we touch a match and it brings us light, a dial and it brings us heat, or cold, or music, or television, never ceases to amaze me.

The fact that I can plant a seed and it becomes a flower, share a bit of knowledge and it becomes another's, smile at someone and receive a smile in return, are to me continual spiritual exercises.

I lecture to a class and find that something I have said affects another's life. I engage in interaction and have the power to create sadness, joy or laughter. Spirituality!

The large varieties of foods creates wonder for me. Oranges, apples, rutabaga, celery, lettuce, hundreds of cuts of differing meats and poultry leave me in a state of bewilderance. A trip to the supermarket staggers me and brings on a state of perceptual overload. The wonder that each food has a distinctive taste, each flower has its own unique features, each day and night has its own music. It is easily apparent that it is not the world that is empty and without wonder — we are.

Magic is not the sole prerogative of the sorcerer. We are ourselves magicians with the power to conjure up and melt away at will. We create the mystery of each day — the secrets lie under every tree, in every insect, in each thought. Flowers will bloom whether we care or not, all foods will have distinctive flavors even if we don't bother to chew or taste them. There will be blazing sunrises even if we never rise early enough to see one. The spirit of each person and thing is present even if we are too asleep to experience it, even if we deny its existence. Spirituality involves an awareness of all there is and an openness to what is not. It is the strength and fearlessness to allow ourselves to transcend reality and ourselves.

Fully functioning individuals know that it is this magic that gives life its spice, irradicates boredom and elevates existence beyond space and time. To be a fully functioning person is to know rapture from an orange and ecstasy in a blade of grass! To be fully functioning is to reach out with total trust and touch the God in all things.

The Role of Frustration and Pain

Every moment of light and dark is a miracle
— Walt Whitman

Fully functioning persons accept emotional pain as an inevitable reality of life. In fact, they take it as an indispensable stimulus for change. This does not mean that they ask for pain or stand passively by waiting to be hurt. Rather, they understand that pain need not only mean discomfort but can also be utilized as a positive force for growth in humanness. A life without pain, if such a life were possible, would be but part of a life; for pain and joy are interrelated, at times dependent one upon the other, in certain circumstances growing one from the other.

The fully functioning person is aware that emotional pain is largely self made. It does not arise, as we so often presume, from the actions of others, a negative situation or an unhappy occurrence. It is our personal reaction to these things. It is not others and other things which cause our unhappiness. It is ourselves. In a very real sense, we are directly responsible for our pain. We may either agonize over our human condition and curse our friends, family, society and God, whom we feel are responsible for it, or we may choose to accept it and do something constructive and personal to ameliorate it. One decision will continue to create useless pain, the other will bring solutions to it. We may feel hopeless depression at the thought of our inevitable old age and death, a depression which will deprive us of present possibilities for life; or we may see the existence of these phenomena as an incentive to improve the quality of our lives now. A personal rejection may be taken as an insurmountable barrier and a reason for self-pity and hate, or as an incentive for looking more closely and critically at our behavior as a means of correcting it and thus, attempting to change the behavior of others toward us. The choices are ours to make. As Nikos Kazantzakas has boldly suggested, "We have our brush and colors — paint Paradise, and in we go." Or, if we so desire, we may create a Hell for ourselves. But if we do choose Hell we must realize that it is of our own choosing and we can, therefore, no longer blame parents, friends, family, society or God. No one and nothing can depress us or cause us pain if we choose not to have it so.

Still, there is much to learn from pain, and since most of us are still not strong enough to healthily reject it, it can still be used for our purposes.

Most people abhor the very idea of pain and see it as a totally negative aspect of existence. They seek to evade it by any means. They perform all types of mental gymnastics, swallow literally tons of pills a day or blind themselves with momentary sources of relief such as alcohol, tranquilizers and drugs. Some, in desperation, will even choose psychosis, a total escape from the painful aspects of reality. They fail to realize that pain can be a dynamic force in helping us to awareness. In fact, I am certain that continuous growth is dependent upon some source of discomfort and that the degree of change is positively related to the degree of pain. Pain is a very human way of demanding change.

When we cling to pain we end up punishing ourselves.

If it were not for physical pain, we would have no idea when we were ill and in physiological jeopardy. We would soon die. Physical pain, though certainly unpleasant, alerts us to the fact that there is a failure in the system which will require immediate attention. If we attend to a toothache at once, we may save the tooth from extraction. If we attempt to ignore the pain, it may momentarily cease to hurt but eventually the tooth will die.

Such is the case with mental pain. If each time we experienced it we would welcome it with interest and give it our immediate attention by asking ourselves, "What is this hurt about?" "What is there for me to learn from it?" "What are my alternative responses besides suffering?", we would perhaps discover the true reason for the pain and be able to arrive at some creative behavioral alternatives to aid ourselves in overcoming it. When we attempt to blame our pain upon others, deny it or sublimate it, we are very likely to find that it has a very clever way of resurfacing and as a result we are experiencing the same pain again and again. I have a friend, for example — a lovely, if lonely, lady — who unwittingly has married the same man, in varying physical forms, five times. Though each marriage has brought her the same despair, she has learned nothing from her desperate encounters. Thus, she is very likely to repeat her error for a sixth time. She has at least one positive factor going for her, she keeps trying.

There are those in even greater danger who experience pain and immediately create protective strategies for the future. They allow themselves to become apathetic, cower in paralyzing fear or retreat from interactions altogether. Once they have identified a specific situation with pain, they will never willfully attempt to experience a similar situation again. They are certain the results will always be the same. Having once been rejected in a love relationship, they are likely to distrust love, become very cautious of tenderness and suspicious of lovers. They may choose isolation, even if their aloneness is more painful than the original rejection.

There are those who cling to pain like a lover, but just as in trying to hold a lover captive, the cost is great. Holding onto pain consumes vast quantities of psychological energies and destroys creativity which could better be spent in active living. Many people have been carrying useless pain around with them for most of their lives, pain which has never been dealt with or resolved and which has, over the years, accumulated strong feelings of bitterness, fear, hate and revenge; this, even after the pain, or its cause, has been forgotten. It has served only to make them suspicious, callous and skeptical. When we cling to pain we end up punishing ourselves.

Fully functioning persons have the courage and strength of their despair. They see it as a positive warning system to alert them to action and change and therefore as an integral part of growth. They know that pain cannot be wished out of existence. It is real, and they must be willing to know it as their own. Having done this and learned from it, they are then free to forgive and let it go forever.

The Role of Intimacy and Love

We are so both and oneful
night cannot be so sky
sky cannot be so sunful
i am through you so i.

— e e cummings

Fully functioning persons recognize their need for others. They do not see this need for love and intimacy as demanding that they be less than they are, but rather as a means for reflecting their vast potentials and sharing them with others. They do not feel restricted by love or intimacy, but see them as a special opportunity for growth. They understand that they can never own another person and have no desire to be so possessed. They know that intimacy brings people together but that it is each person's responsibility to maintain autonomy; that they must grow separately in order to continue to grow with others. Love and intimacy are challenged, not threatened by differences. Fully functioning persons know that when two separate individuals decide to form an intimate relationship, they are uniting two different worlds, and, as such, not only bring to each other only commonalities, but differences. It is the differences which will continue to stimulate them to growth. The depth of our love can usually be measured by the degree to which we are willing to share ourselves with others. We begin with separate *I*'s. We set up a shared space between the two *I*'s and call it *us*. It is this space where intimacy grows. The greater the shared experience the more the area of *us*.

Love and intimacy have many stages and therefore will be constantly changing. The intimacy of the first meeting will not be the intimacy of the honeymoon, but there will be many honeymoons; the honeymoon of the first one-bedroom apartment with its borrowed furniture; the honeymoon of the first child; the honeymoon of the down payment on a first home; the honeymoon of the first significant promotion; the honeymoon of growing with the family, watching the children form their own families; the honeymoon of growing old together. Each honeymoon will be new and will create further depths of intimacy. It is therefore imperative that the fully functioning person be constantly aware and open to change. The person in one's arms today will not be the same person tomorrow, or even, for that matter, in the next hour. Love is not nurtured or enhanced by looking back, it is always lived in the now.

Mature intimacy and love are not based upon expectations. Since no one, not even a saint, can know or meet all of our expectations, to expect from others is to court pain and disappointment. The only valid expectation in love lies in the hope that those we love will become themselves, as we do the same. Love given out of a sense of duty or obligation, is the greatest insult and therefore not love at all.

Real love and intimacy grow best in spontaneity and offer an abundance of opportunities for experiences of joy, beauty and laughter. We have all known the wonder of sharing a peak experience with another, whether of laughter or pain. For a moment the shared experience has taken two and made them one. These moments of deep intimacy will continue to make love more refreshing, exciting and youthful.

Mature intimacy, as suggested earlier, involves the physical. Integral to it seems to be a sensual need to be near the loved ones, to make contact physically, to hold them, and keep them close. Therefore, it will require that the fully functioning persons first come to terms with their own sexuality. We must feel comfortable with our own sexual self before we can risk revealing our sexuality freely and honestly to another. This does not mean that we desire to be overtly sexual with everyone with whom we are growing in love. In a broader sense it refers to sexual gratification in which we may be satisfied by merely being in the same space with another, holding our child, deeply sharing with a friend.

There is perhaps no more natural, nor more totally satisfying action of which the human person is capable than that which is found in a mature sexual intimacy. Here, in its highest form, lies a deep desire to totally merge with another. It is an ultimate expression of love combining all of its positive manifestations — caring, giving, sharing, nurturing, confirming, accepting, yielding and assuming. Sexuality, when an expression of one's real love, can be the ultimate human unity.

Love and intimacy require some verbal expression. Too often we assume that the other person or persons *know* what we are thinking or how we are feeling. We are often surprised when we discover that this is not true. It is the lover's responsibility to reach out and touch the heart of the loved one — a word, a note, a flower, a simple poem, can bring the much needed message of assurance. One never tires of knowing love expressed.

Love and intimacy require compassion. Unless we are able to feel with the other, we are unable to love. This does not mean that we can completely empathize with another's feelings and behaviors. It is painful to me when I hear someone say, "I know just how you feel!" One does not! One never can! At best, we are able to understand only what we have truly experienced, and each experience is always very personal. But when we have a knowledge of our own personal conflicts and feelings based upon general human experience we can begin to understand how others may feel. It is this point at which compassion begins.

Love and intimacy have no place for exploitation. There is an old statement, but still true, "Use things, love people." It is frightening how many individuals do just the opposite in the name of love: parents who use their children, husbands who use their wives, educators who use their students, radicals who use their society. They use the lives of others to affirm their own being and worth. This is basically why love has become such a questionable and frightening concept. It is so often used to violate rather than stimulate. Exploitation, in a relationship, no matter how we rationalize it, can never be love!

Perfect human love is difficult to find. We seem to have few models to look toward. But the behaviors which seem to enhance love are consistent, observable and available for study. Fully functioning persons know that it must be mainly self-taught, and it is best learned through simply being vulnerable to love and by living in it as dedicated human lovers each day of our lives.

The implication in this chapter is not that we need to be perfect to be fully functioning in personhood. The contrary is true. Perfection suggests an ultimate state, a completion, a termination. The fully functioning human person does not seek this, even in death.

THE CHALLENGE TO YOUR FULL FUNCTIONING PERSONHOOD

First of all, although men have a common destiny, each individual also has to work out his own personal salvation for himself in fear and trembling. We can help one another to find the meaning of life no doubt. But in the last analysis, the individual person is responsible for living his own life and for "finding himself." If he persists in shifting his responsibility to somebody else, he fails to find out the meaning of his own existence. You cannot tell me who I am, and I cannot tell you who you are. If you do not know your own identity, who is going to identify you?

— Thomas Merton

CHAPTER 5

Since there are no limits to the potential of personhood, there can be no end to this work. What we have shared here is but a clumsy beginning, a fumbling through the myriad of intricacies and wonder that make up the human person. Like the society in which we live, we are a mass of joyful contradictions, complexities, imperfections, incertitudes and magic. The search for full humanness is in the process of trying to make some personal sense of the contradictions, of attempting to unravel the seeming complexities, of struggling with the imperfections, of overcoming the incertitudes and of actively reveling in the magic.

We are being told that personhood and its actualization are becoming obsolete as are the phenomena of life and death and their inherent struggles. Modern science assures us it will soon be able to reproduce the perfect person in the laboratory and program it for life according to a pre-prescribed model of anatomical perfection. At the same time, educators are questioning the ability of the human being to deal with such values as freedom and dignity and are busily devising plans for programmed learning which, they assure us, through experimental design, will rid us of the conflict-inducing illusion of our uniqueness and individuality. In its place they are ready to substitute a type of lifelong contentment for all. They assure us that it is our dream of personhood that is at the root of all human problems and that if we are willing to relinquish that dream they will rid us of further pain, conflict and anxiety.

But I am optimistic. I like being a human being. Even with all my frailties, abilities to hurt, forget, cause conflicts, know

We have a powerful survival instinct, an intense desire to live. How else would we have endured so many centuries of enslavement, hunger, pain, imprisonment and struggle and still have emerged choosing life?

pain and feel fear, I am delighted with life. And, even if this life I am living is an illusion, as they assure me it is, at least it is an exciting illusion and one of my own making! In addition, I am convinced that Personkind is more like me than different. They are not so easily duped, nor can they be so easily convinced of their uselessness and impotence. We have a powerful survival instinct, an intense desire to live. How else would we have endured so many centuries of enslavement, hunger, pain, imprisonment and struggle and still have emerged choosing life?

Personhood is not a gift, it is an inalienable right. We have a rightful place on this earth and in this universe. We have had enough of alienation. We are weary of being fragmented and living under the constant threat of annihilation. All things considered, we're not too bad.

Our desire is to be made whole again. We want to experience life with even more intensity than before, and more holistically, with our entire mind, body and spirit. We want to make our life a celebration. Our history, as we are too often reminded, may not have been the most joyous or encouraging, but we are not irrevocably tied to our past. We want to participate in the process of creating a more perfect now.

We are far from disheartened. Each of us still has within us that which is necessary to remake the world. The principle motivational force necessary to accomplish this requires only our personal commitment to dedicate ourselves to the process of living our lives fully, not only to exist in life, but to experience it totally. Our lives are original documents which we alone can create. Either we create them or they will never exist.

The individual power is within each of us. It is ours to draw upon whenever we wish. It never dies. It simply lies dormant until *we* come to life. It is not mysterious. It is realized daily, each time we are fully aware and engaging enthusiastically and with abandon in the process of living.

So is our challenge. It is obvious that it is a very personal challenge which each of us can meet only for ourselves, yet all of us must do so to give each other's life validity.

For some of us it will be a struggle necessitating new learning. For others it will be the equally difficult task of unlearning what has already been learned but which no longer serves our growth. For most, it will require both. Whichever the way, none will be particularly easy. It will be a bit more simple, though, if we do not attempt to accomplish all of our goals in one day.

Life is always ready and open at our side to share its resources. It simply awaits our embrace. It offers us our choices, approves our decisions and walks in our direction. It is continuously forgiving, amazingly adjustable, always accepting and forever encouraging. It is willing at any given moment to start afresh. It attempts always to guide us toward becoming our fully functioning and active selves, for in this way it can enhance itself. Only life, after all, begets life.

There is nothing to fear. Hemingway said, "Man was not made for defeat. Man can be destroyed, but not defeated." Armed with life on our side and a lifetime to experiment, the odds are in our favor.

Your Personhood is real. It is your most valuable possession. It can be known, experienced and felt. No one can suffer its loss more desperately than you. As long as it remains in life it can endlessly grow, develop and change. Its genesis is a miracle, which for a moment takes on the form called *you*, then passes on its way. To devalue the miracle is your most unforgivable crime. To keep it from actualizing itself is to forfeit your role in the necessary process of life recreating itself.

At one time in my life I decided that I wanted to learn the art of Japanese brush painting. I immediately sought a famous teacher, purchased all the necessary materials and arranged for regular classes. I was impatient to produce one of those simple four or five stroke masterpieces which I had seen Japanese masters produce in a matter of minutes with such wondrous results as Butterfly on Bamboo Branch or Persimmon in Moonlight.

You can imagine my disappointment when, several months later, my teacher was still insisting upon nothing more than straight brush strokes across a white page — one following the other in rows of twenty — each of the same texture, thickness and "feeling." Where was my butterfly? My persimmon? That, he assured me, would come in time. For now and for months to come, I was to concentrate on making simple straight lines.

To master an art requires time, the understanding of and sensitivity for the materials necessary, and extreme patience while the basic skills are being learned. It includes the willingness to experiment, to fail, to risk, to know frustration and even despair before one can abandon learned parroted techniques and project oneself fully in self-creation. To be an artist of life requires no less.

Meister Eckart, an astonishingly perceptive Christian philosopher of the 13th century, stated "The shell must be cracked apart if what is in it is to come out, for if you want to know the kernel you must break the shell."

I have attempted here to break the shell. It is hoped that the kernel lies a bit more exposed for our study. There, among its parts, are to be found our ally, in death; our hope, in self-creation; our strength, in connectiveness; our uniqueness, in purpose; our rapture, in intimacy and love; and the source for overcoming our doubts, frustrations and pain. There is much still to be found. Comfort lies in the fact that the first step is taken.

The shell has been cracked apart, the kernel is exposed awaiting you.

Trying the Empty Nothing, and
demanding something;
Banging the Silent Zero, in search
of sound.

139

REFERENCES

1. Maslow AH: The Farther Reaches of Human Nature. New York, Viking Press Inc, 1971.
2. Gandhi MK: Autobiography, The Story of My Experiments with Truth. Boston, Beacon Press, 1957, p 338.
3. Linneberg EH: On explaining language. Science 164, No. 3880, 1969.
4. Norton DL: Personal Destinies. Princeton, Princeton University Press, 1976.
5. Rogers C: On Becoming a Person. New York, Houghton-Mifflin Co., 1961, pp 187-192.
6. Nasr SH: Ideals and Realities of Islam. Boston, Beacon Press, 1972.

BIBLIOGRAPHY

This is a short bibliography of books which have been important in my journey to grow in personhood. It is by no means exhaustive, and I feel sure that there are several titles which have served their purpose and have since been forgotten; therefore, they are sadly not included here.

There are other works which the reader might add to the list and I welcome them. This bibliography, like this entire work, is but a beginning.

Leo Buscaglia.

Allport G: On Becoming: Basic Considerations for a Psychology of Personality. New Haven, Conn, Yale University Press, 1955.

Assagioli R: Psychosynthesis: A Manual of Principals and Techniques. New York, Viking Press Inc, 1972.

Assagioli R: The Act Of Will. New York, Viking Press Inc, 1973. (New York, Penguin Books Inc, 1974.)

Axline VM: Dibs: In Search Of Self. New York, Penguin Books Inc, 1971.

Baba Ram Das: Be Here Now. New York, Crown Pub Inc, 1971.

Berne E: What Do You Say After You Say Hello? New York, Grove Press Inc, 1972. (New York, Bantam Basic Books Inc, 1973.)

Bettelheim B: The Informal Heart: Autonomy in a Mass Age. New York, Free Press, 1960. (New York, Avon Books, 1971.)

Bettelheim B: Love Is Not Enough. New York, Free Press, 1950.

Blakney B (ed): Meister Eckhart: A Modern Translation. New York, Harper & Row Pub Inc, 1941.

Buber M: Between Man & Man. New York, Macmillan Pub Co Inc, 1965.

Buddhadasa: Toward the Truth. Philadelphia, Westminister Press, 1971.

Camus A: The Myth of Sisyphus and Other Essays. New York, Alfred A Knopf Inc, 1955.

Camus A: The Stranger. New York, Alfred A. Knopf Inc, 1946.

Castaneda C: Tales of Power. Simon & Schuster Inc, 1975.

Chaudhuri H: Integral Yoga. Wheaton, Illinois, Theosophical Publishing House, 1974.

Chung-yuan C: Creativity and Taoism. New York, Julian Press Inc, 1963.

Dubos R: Beast or Angel? Choices That Make Us Human. New York, Charles Scribner's Sons, 1974.

Egner RE, Denonn LE (eds): The Basic Writings of Bertrand Russell. New York, Simon & Schuster Inc, 1961.

Eiseley L: Firmament of Time. New York, Atheneum Pub, 1960.

Eiseley L: The Immense Journey. New York, Random House Inc, 1957.

Erickson EH: Childhood and Society. New York, WW Norton & Co Inc, 1964.

de Saint Exupery A: The Little Prince. New York, Harcourt Brace Javonovich Inc, 1971.

Fromm E: Man For Himself: An Inquiry Into the Psychology of Ethics. New York, Holt Rinehart & Winston, 1947. (New York, Fawcett World Library, 1968.)

Fromm E: The Art of Loving. New York, Harper & Row Pub Inc, 1956.

Gasset O: On Love. Elnora, New York, Meridian Press, 1957.

Gasset O: Man and Crisis. New York, WW Norton & Co Inc, 1962.

Gasset O: Man and People. New York, WW Norton & Co Inc, 1963.

Gibran K: The Prophet. New York, Alfred A Knopf Inc, 1972.

Gillies J: Friends. New York, Coward McCann & Geoghegan Inc, 1976.

Hammarskjold Dag: Markings. New York, Alfred A Knopf Inc, 1964.

Harper R: Human Love: Existential and Mystical. Baltimore, Maryland, Johns Hopkins Press, 1966.

Hesse H: Demian. New York, Harper & Row Pub Inc, 1965.

Hesse H: Siddartha. New York, Bantam Books Inc, 1976.

Jourard S: The Transparent Self, ed 2. New York, Van Nostrand Reinhold Co, 1971.

Jourard S, Overlade DC: Disclosing Man to Himself: The Task of Humanistic Psychology. New York, Van Nostrand Reinhold Co, 1968.

Jung CG: Man and His Symbols. New York, Dell Pub Co, 1970.

Jung CG: Memories, Dreams, Reflections. New York, Vintage Books, 1963.

Jung CG: Modern Man in Search of a Soul. New York, Harcourt Brace & World, 1962.

Jung CG: The Portable Jung. New York, Viking Press, 1971.

Kapleau P: The Three Pillars of Zen. Boston, Beacon Press Inc, 1967.

Kazantzakis N: The Saviors of God. New York, Simon & Schuster Inc, 1960.

Kubler Ross E: Death: The Final Stage of Growth. Englewood Cliffs, NJ, Prentice-Hall Inc, 1975.

Kubler Ross E: Images of Growth and Death. Englewood Cliffs, NJ, Prentice-Hall Inc, 1976.

Laing RD: Politics of Experience. New York, Ballantine Books Inc, 1976.

Leonard G: Education and Ecstasy. New York, Dell Pub Co, 1968.

Lindberg AM: Bring Me a Unicorn: Diaries and Letters of Anne Morrow Lindberg. New York, Harcourt Brace Javonovich Inc, 1972.

Lindberg AM: Gifts from the Sea. New York, Random House Inc, 1955.

Maslow A: Motivation and Personality, rev ed. New York, Harper & Row Pub Inc, 1970.

Maslow A: Religions, Values and Peak Experiences. New York, Viking Press Inc, 1970.

Maslow A: Toward a Psychology of Being, ed 2. New York, Van

Nostrand Reinhold Co, 1968.

Matson F: The Idea of Man. New York, Delacorte Press, 1976.

Matson F, Montagu A (eds): Human Dialogue. New York, Free Press, 1967.

May R: Love and Will. New York, WW Norton & Co Inc, 1969. (New York, Dell Pub Co, 1973.)

May R: Man's Search for Himself. New York, WW Norton & Co Inc, 1953. (New York, Dell Pub Co, 1973.)

May R: Psychology and the Human Dilemma. New York, Van Nostrand Reinholt Co, 1966.

Merton T: Conjectures of a Guilty Bystander. New York, Doubleday & Co Inc, 1968.

Merton T: Mystics and Zen Masters. New York, Dell Pub Co, 1969.

Merton T: No Man Is an Island. New York, Doubleday & Co Inc.

Merton T: Zen and the Birds of Appetite. Abbey of Gethsemani Inc, 1968.

Morris C: Varieties of Human Value. Chicago, University of Chicago Press, 1965.

Moustakas CE: Loneliness. Englewood Cliffs, NJ, Prentice-Hall Inc, 1961.

Moustakas CE: Personal Growth: The Struggle for Identity and Human Values. Cambridge, MA, Howard A Doyle Pub Co, 1969.

Moustakas CE: Portraits of Loneliness and Love. Englewood Cliffs, NJ, Prentice-Hall Inc, 1974.

Murphy G: Human Potentialities. New York, Basic Books Inc, 1958.

Ornstein R: Psychology of Consciousness. New York, Viking Press Inc, 1973.

Otto H: Ways of Growth: Approaches to Expanding Awareness. New York, Grossman Pub Co, 1968. (New York, Pocket Books Inc, 1971.)

Paulus T: Hope for the Flowers. Paramus, NJ, Paulist/Newman Press, 1972.

Pearce J: The Crack in the Cosmic Egg. New York, Julian Press Inc, 1971. (New York, Pocket Books Inc, 1973.)

Pearce JC: Magical Child. New York, EP Dutton & Co Inc, 1977.

Perls FS: In and Out of the Garbage Pail. Moab, UT, Real People Press, 1969.

Priestley JB: Man and Time. New York, Dell Pub Co Inc, 1964.

Reik T: The Need to Be Loved. New York, Farrar Strauss & Giroux Inc, 1963.

Reps P (ed): Zen Flesh and Zen Bones. Rutland, VT, CE Tuttle Co Inc, 1957.

Reps P: Be! New York, John Weatherhill Inc, 1971.

Rogers C: On Becoming A Person. Boston, MA, Houghton Mifflin Co, 1961.

Rogers C, Stevens B: Person to Person: The Problem of Being Human. Moab, UT, Real People Press, 1967.

Roosevelt E: Autobiography of Eleanor Roosevelt. New York, Harper & Row Pub Co, 1961.

Roosevelt E: This I Remember. Westport, CT, Grennwood Press Inc, 1975.

Roosevelt E: You Learn by Living. New York, Harper & Row Pub Co, 1960.

Ross NW: The World of Zen. New York, Random House Inc, 1960.

Russell B: The Conquest of Happiness. New York, Liveright Pub Corp, 1930.

Samples R, Wohlford R: Opening: A Primer for Self Actualization. Reading, MA, Addison-Wesley Pub Co, 1974.

Sartre JP: Being and Nothingness. Secaucus, NJ, Citadel Press, 1964.

Satir V: Peoplemaking. Palo Alto, CA, Science & Behavior Books Inc, 1972.

Schultz W: Joy: Expanding Human Awareness. New York, Grove Press Inc, 1967. (New York, Ballentine Books Inc, 1973.)

Schweitzer A: Albert Schweitzer: An Anthology. New York, Harper & Row Pub Inc, 1947.

Schweitzer A: Light Within Us. Secaucus, NJ, Citadel Press, 1959.

Schweitzer A: Pilgrimage to Humanity. Philosophy Library, 1961.

Selye H: Stress of Life. New York, McGraw Hill Book Co, 1956.

Shah I: Wisdom of the Idiots. New York, EP Dutton & Co Inc, 1971.

Skinner BF: Walden Two. New York, Macmillan Pub Co Inc, 1969.

Sorokin PA: Ways and Power of Love. Chicago, Henry Regnery Co, 1967.

Steven B: Don't Push the River. Moab, UT, Real People Press, 1970.

Storm H: Seven Arrows. New York, Ballantine Books Inc, 1973.

Suzuki DT: Zen Buddhism. New York, Doubleday & Co Inc, 1956.

Teilhard De Chardin P: Phenomenon of Man. New York, Harper & Row Pub Inc, 1959.

Tillich P: Courage to Be. New Haven, CT. Yale University Press, 1952.

Tzu L: The Way of Life. New York, Capricorn Books, 1962.

Watts A: The Book: On The Taboo of Knowing Who You Are. New York, Pantheon Books, 1966. (New York, Random House Inc, 1974.)

Watts A: The Way of Zen. New York, Random House Inc, 1974.

Wiesel E: Souls on Fire; Portraits and Legends of Hasidic Masters. New York, Random House Inc, 1973.

Yogananda P: Autobiography of a Yogi. Los Angeles, Self Realization Fellowship, 1971.

Personhood is not a gift, it is an inalienable right.

DATE DUE

Jun. - 6 1991	JUL 2 4 1991	MAR 2 1 1992	JUN 0 7 1994	MAR 2 1 1995	JUN - 4 1996	JAN 1 6 1997	JUN. 2 5 1999	1/14/15	
	SEP 2 3 1991		3 1994	MAY 2 2	DEC 2 6 1996	JAN 3 0 1998			
JUN 1 1 1985	OCT 8 - 1985	JUL 2 8 1986	SEP 2 3 1986	FEB 2 5 1987	SEP - 9 1987 JUL 2 3	AUG 6 - 1988	JAN	FEB 1 6 1990	OCT 1 7 1990